Beaded Bracelets Pattern Collection

Sandra D. Halpenny

Beaded Bracelets Pattern Collection

Published by: Sandra D. Halpenny
Copyright © 2011, Sandra D. Halpenny

Canadian Intellectual Property Office,
Beaded Bracelets Pattern Collection,
2011 Certificate of Copyright Registration #1084076
Bracelet Pattern Collection,
2007 Certificate of Copyright Registration #1046514

Beaded Bracelets Pattern Collection
Revised Edition 2011
ISBN 978-1456592370
ISBN-10: 1456592378

Editor: Rosalie Wakefield
Patterns proofed and tested by: Julia Wentz

Bracelet Designs, Illustrations and Photographs,
Copyright © 2011, Sandra D. Halpenny

All rights reserved. No part of this book, text, photographs or illustrations, may be reproduced or transmitted in any way known now or as yet unknown, without written permission obtained beforehand from the author.

Every effort has been made to ensure that all the information in this book is accurate. However, due to differing conditions, tools and individual skills, the publisher cannot be responsible for any injuries, losses or other damages that may result from the use of the information in this book.

The finished items made from this book can be made for personal use and for individual's own pin money. You have my permission to make and sell the finished bracelets at arts and craft shows, etc. No MASS production allowed. You may NOT teach classes from this book without written permission from the author. You may NOT distribute the patterns from this book in any way.

http://www.SandraDHalpenny.com

TABLE OF CONTENTS

Getting Started with Bead Weaving.................4

Sky Blue Bracelet..................................10

Gold Time Bracelet................................14

Aqua Lace Bracelet................................20

Emerald Lace Bracelet............................24

Crystal Lace Bracelet.............................28

Aqua Luster Bracelet..............................32

Gunmetal Iris Bracelet............................38

Crystal Edge Bracelet.............................42

Magenta Bronze Bracelet........................46

Lilac Blue Bracelet.................................50

Fuchsia Blue Bracelet.............................56

Gold Wine Bracelet................................60

Crystal Explosion Bracelet......................68

Olive Lace Bracelet................................74

Getting Started with Bead Weaving

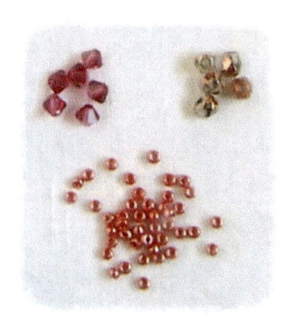

Beads

All my patterns are designed using Japanese seed beads. I like to use the Japanese seed beads because they are uniform in size and the holes are large and even and wide enough to go through with thread several times. Of course, you can use any kind of seed beads, some of the patterns might need to be adjusted. Do a small section first, to see how your seed beads will work.

Thread

What you would look for is a beading thread with a weight of D. My favorites are Nymo and C-Lon thread. This is a thread that is not too heavy and not too thin. Match the color of thread to the color of beads that are in your bracelet.

I have recently started using Fireline® fishing line, too. I like 4lb and 6lb for bead weaving. You do not need to stretch or wax it.

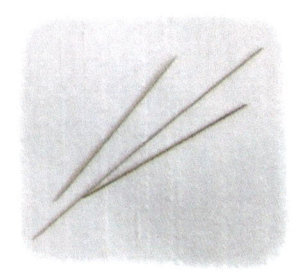

Needles

Beading needles come in different lengths and sizes. You will need sizes #11 and #12 beading needles. They come in short and long versions. I use the John James sharps. I prefer the short, but it really makes no difference if you use either one.

Beeswax

Beeswax is used for conditioning your thread. It can also help to keep your thread from tangling. You can get it from any bead store and also from any fabric store. The fabric stores usually sell beeswax in a round plastic container.

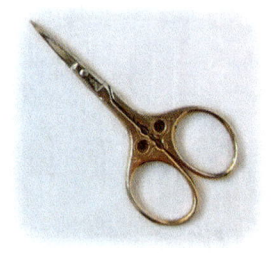

Scissors

You will need a small, very sharp scissors. Invest in a good one, it is worth it.

Clear Nail Polish

No we are not going to do our nails. Nail polish is used for holding your knots and your thread in place. Only use fresh clear polish. Note: If you are using dyed beads, check for color fastness before using the polish. Sometimes nail polish can remove color from beads.

Portable Work Area

This is how I move around the house with what I am working on.

I first start with a lap desk. This is a flat board, about 12" x 10", attached to a pillow. Cut a piece of no-slip vinyl shelf liner to fit (this keeps the tray in place, even if you have to get up really fast) and put that on the lap desk. Then a tray, you do not want the tray to have edges that are too high, otherwise it will bother your arm if you are working on your lap.

Then put another piece of shelf liner and finally a placemat. I use a tightly woven placemat, so the beads don't get lost in the texture of the fabric. It also keeps the beads from bouncing at you when you are working. If I am working at a table, I just use the tray part, if I am working on my lap, I use the whole set up.

This is how I lay out my work surface. I bring the needle to the beads on the tray when picking up, not the beads to the needle. The little silver spoon I use for scooping up beads to put them away.

Terminology

These are the terms that I use.

Each pattern tells you the type of beads that are used for the pattern.

A = 11° seed beads
B = 4mm bi-cone crystals

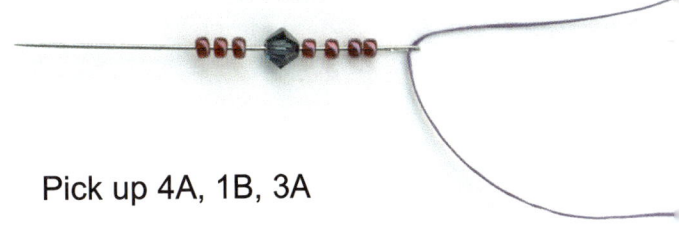

Pick up 4A, 1B, 3A

Pick up
Pick up, is used for the amount and type of beads that you pick up on your working needle and thread. The picture above shows,
Pick up 4A, 1B, 3A

Go with thread
Go with thread refers to your working thread and needle.

getting started 5

go forward **go down** **go up**

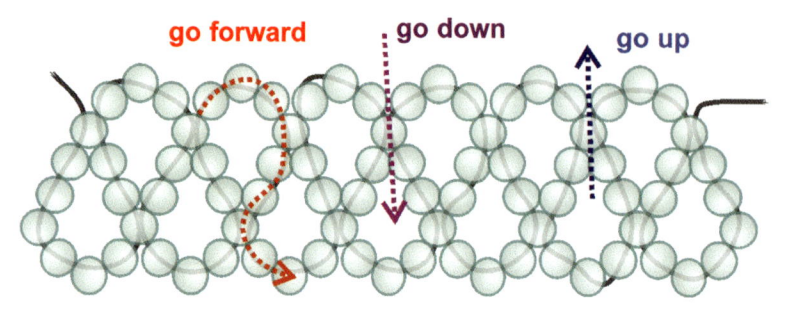

go forward, go up, go down
Go forward, is to go with your working thread and needle in the same direction as all the steps have gone. Up and down are simply up or down.

To Start

Cut about 1 yard of thread. When you get more experienced, you can start with a longer thread. When you cut the thread, cut it on an angle, this makes it easier to thread into the needle.

Run the thread through the beeswax a couple of times. Then run the thread through your fingers and stretch the thread as you are rubbing off the excess wax. DO NOT skip the stretching of the thread part. This is a big mistake that beginners make, including myself when I began. What can happen if you don't stretch the thread, after awhile the thread will start to stretch on it's own with the weight of the beads and the tension will become too loose. As you are working, keep in mind your tension. You don't want the tension too tight, but you also don't want to see the thread.

Thread your beading needle. Hint: Pinch the thread between you thumb and finger, then bring the thread to the needle hole. Beading needle holes are very small, so it takes a bit of patience when you first start to thread them.

Whether using thread or fishing line, for ease in threading the beading needle use a permanent marker and touch the tip of the thread. The marker makes the end of the thread more visible and it also stiffens the end of the thread so that it goes more easily into the needle hole.

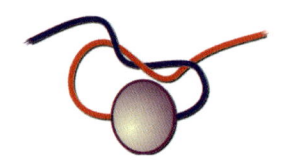

Now you need to **add a stopper bead** to the end of the working thread. I use an overhand knot, so the bead will hold, but will also slide off easily. This bead can be a different color. The stopper bead is used to hold your beads on while you working on your piece and helps to keep your tension.

Pick up the stopper bead, slide it down to the end of your working thread, leaving at least an 8" tail. With the thread, make a loop over your stopper bead bringing the left end thread over and through the back of the right hand thread. Pull up ends so the thread is snug around the stopper bead.

When you are done, you can pull off the stopper bead by putting the blunt end of your needle through the bead and pull it off by sliding down the thread tail.

Abbreviations:

FT = first time only
ETA = every time after

6 beaded bracelets pattern collection

Bringing in new thread, and ending the old thread

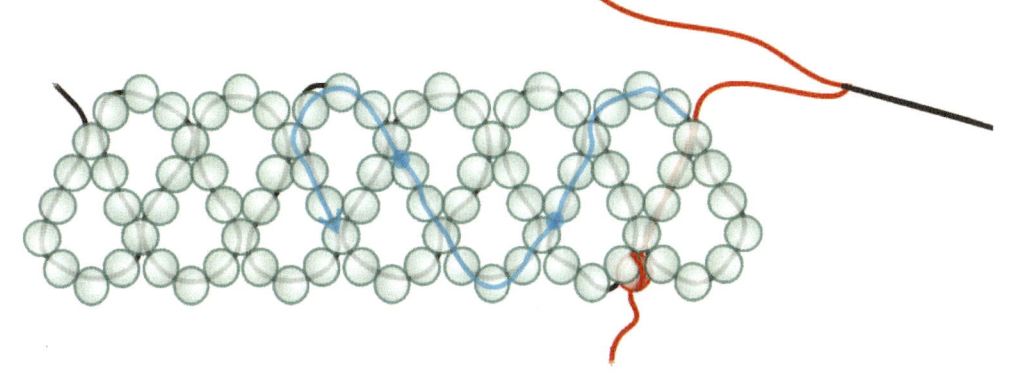

When you start to run out of thread or if you see that your working thread is starting to fray, it is time to bring a new thread in and end the old thread.

The light blue line in the illustration represents the finished working thread. Go with thread back though several beads in your bead weaving. Make a half hitch knot (shown in illustration as light blue dots). Weave through again with your working thread several more beads and make another half hitch knot, but before pulling up the thread to tighten the knot, put a bit of the clear nail polish on the knot area and about 1/4" along the thread. Pull up the knot tight and continue with the working thread through several more beads in your piece. Trim off the thread as close as possible to the beads.

Please note: If your piece has more than one row, you can weave the working thread through the beads and leave it without putting in the knot until the next row is complete. If you make a knot, and you need to go through the bead where the knot is, the bead hole will be blocked. You can go back later to do the knotting. You never want to force the needle though beads, the beads are made of glass and can be broken.

The red line in the illustration represents bringing in a new thread with a stopper bead. The stopper bead can be removed after several steps have been completed in the pattern. Pull off the stopper bead and weave off the end of the new thread in the opposite direction of the old thread.

The Half Hitch Knot

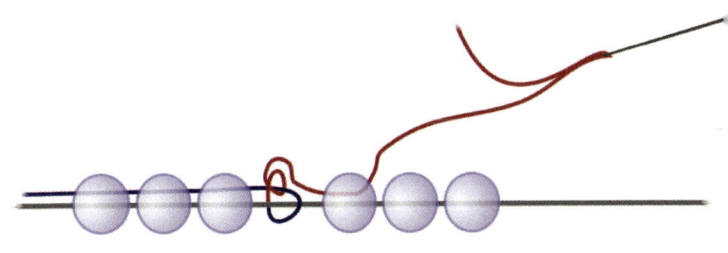

To make a half hitch knot, go around the thread in the piece with your working thread and needle between 2 beads.
Make a loop and go through the loop in the working thread, pull up to tighten.
Please note: When weaving your threads through areas that already have been done, try not to split the threads with your working needle, it can weaken the strength of your threads.

Adding Clasp

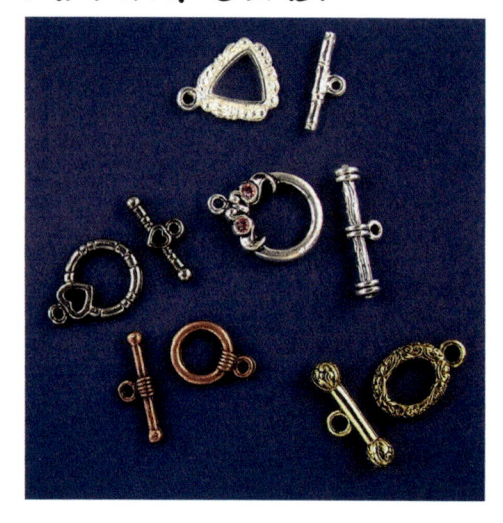

There are many kind of clasps available, from very expensive to very cheap. For bracelets I especially like using toggle closures. Always try to match your toggle to your bracelet. Don't use a cheap toggle for a bracelet that has taken you many hours to complete and has expensive beads in it.

To add a toggle

With the working thread from the bracelet, pick up 7 seed beads, go with thread through 1, 2 or 3 beads in bracelet, forward through the first 4 beads added for closure, go through the loop on the toggle, back through the 4th bead, go again through the toggle. Continue doing this until the 4th bead is full of thread. Weave the working thread into the bracelet and end. Continue with your working thread around and through all the clasp beads several times.

Repeat in the same manner at the other end after removing the stopper bead. Use the stopper bead tail thread to add the other end of the clasp.

My Favorite Toggle,

Beaded toggle and loop closure

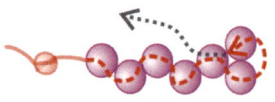

1. To make the toggle, Start a new thread, add a stopper bead, leaving a 10" tail. Rows 1 and 2: Pick up 6 seed beads and slide them up next to the stopper bead.

2. Row 3: Pick up 1 seed bead, skip over the 1st seed bead, go with thread, right to left through the next seed bead and pull up thread so the beads are stacked on top of each other as shown in drawing.

3. Row 4: Pick up 1 seed bead, skip over 1 seed bead, go with thread, left to right through the next seed bead in Row 3, pull up thread.

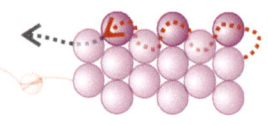

4. Row 5: Pick up 1 seed bead, skip over 1 seed bead, go with thread right to left through the next seed bead in Row 3, pull up thread.

8 beaded bracelets pattern collection

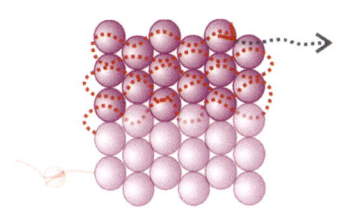

5. Rows 6, 7, 8, 9 and 10, repeat steps 5 or 6 to make 5 more rows.

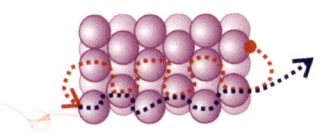

6. Roll the small piece into a tube. With the working thread, weave across from the 10th row into the 1st row, going back and forth between the beads like a zipper. With the working thread weave through the beads in the tube, so your thread can come out the other end.

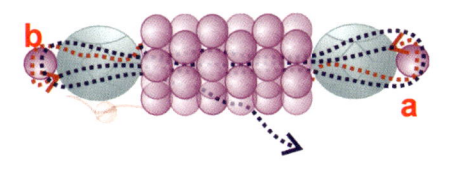

7. a) Pick up 1 crystal (to match bracelet) and 1 seed bead, go with thread back down through the crystal and the center of the tube.
b) Pick up 1 crystal and 1 seed bead, go with thread back down through the crystal and the center of the tube. Continue with thread as many times going through the beads added in step #10 and #11 and the center of the tube. When you can't go through the beads any more, Continue with thread into the beads in the tube and end the thread. Toggle made.

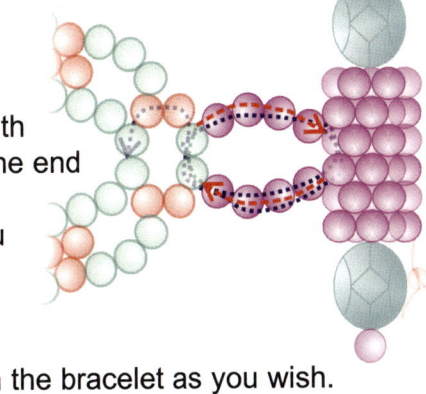

9. Pick up 4 beads, go with thread into the end beads in the bracelet. You can go through as many or as few beads in the bracelet as you wish. If there is a crystal at the end, go through the crystal and 1 or 2 seed beads. Pick up 4 beads, go with thread through 2 seed beads in the middle of the toggle. Continue with thread around through all these beads as many times as you can. When done, weave thread into the bracelet and end.

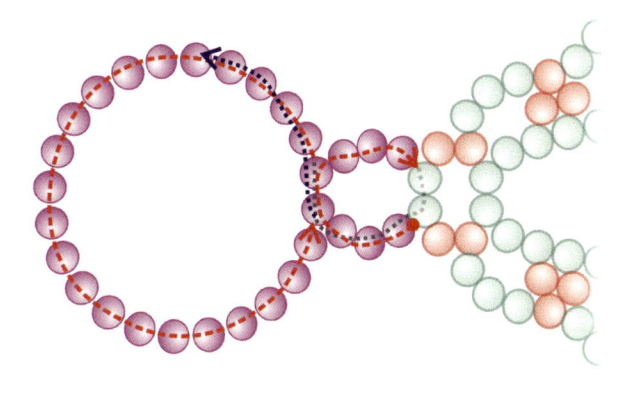

10. To make the loop, remove the stopper bead on the bracelet, put the end thread on your needle. Pick up 8 seed beads and go with thread through andy seed beads in the bracelet. Continue with thread around and through the 1st through 5th seed beads just added. Pick up 20 - 23 seed beads (make a loop with the beads to see if they fit over the toggle), go with thread down through the 4th and 5th seed beads in the previous loop you just made. Check again to make sure the loop fits over the toggle. Continue with thread through all the loop beads as many times as you can. When done, weave thread into the bracelet and end.

my favorite toggle 9

Sky Blue Bracelet

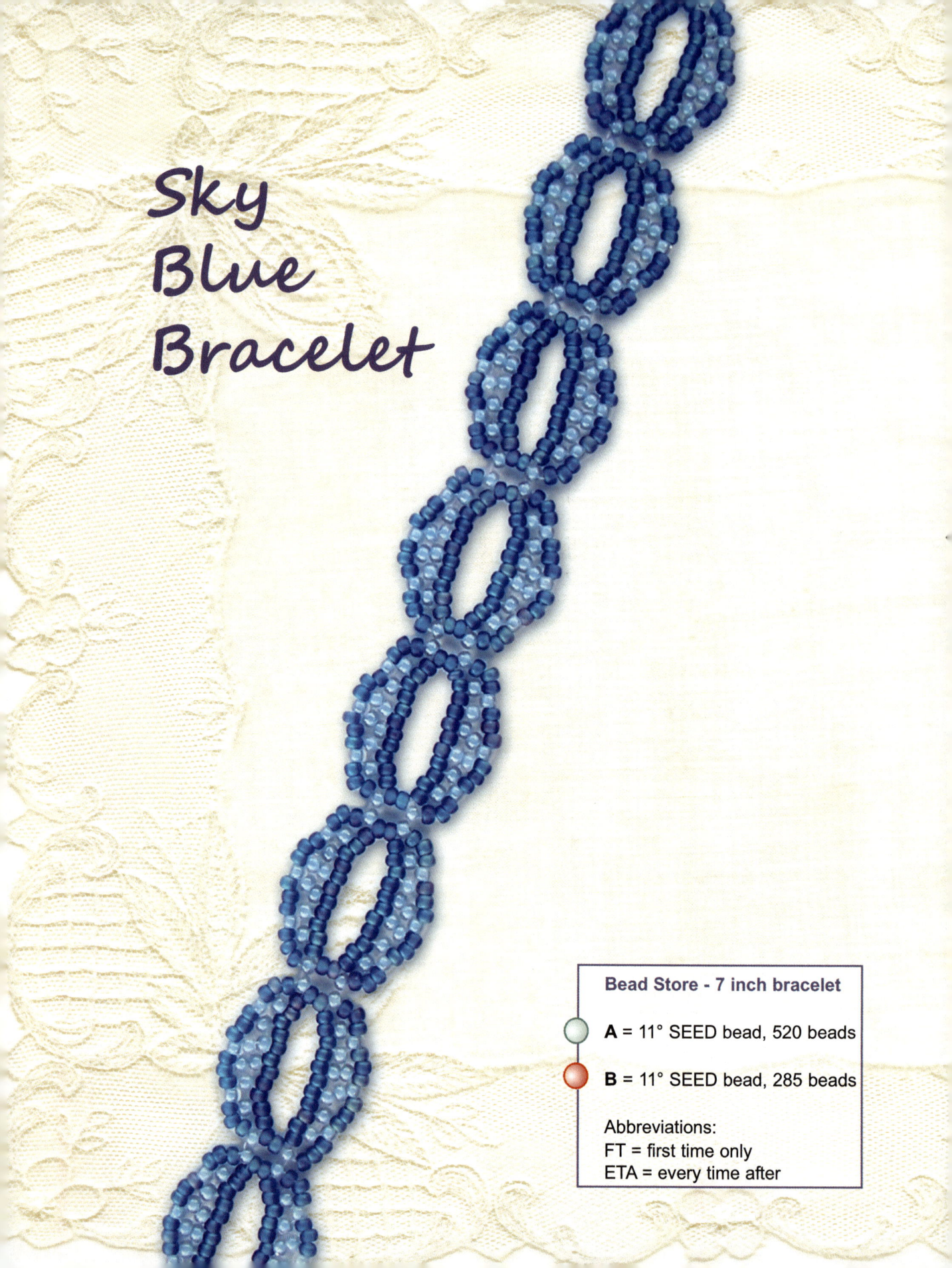

Bead Store - 7 inch bracelet

○ **A** = 11° SEED bead, 520 beads

○ **B** = 11° SEED bead, 285 beads

Abbreviations:
FT = first time only
ETA = every time after

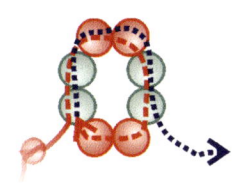

1. Pick up 2A, 2B, 2A, 2B, go with thread forward through the 2 A, 2 B and 2 A beads just added.

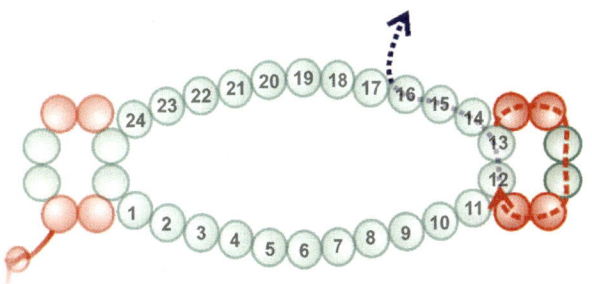

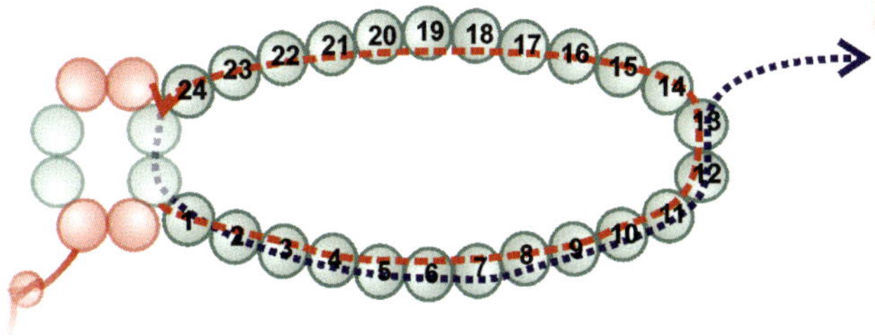

2. Pick up 24A, go with thread down through the 2nd set of 2 A beads added in step #1 (FT) or the 2 A beads added in step #3 (ETA) and forward through the 1st through 13th A beads just added in this step.

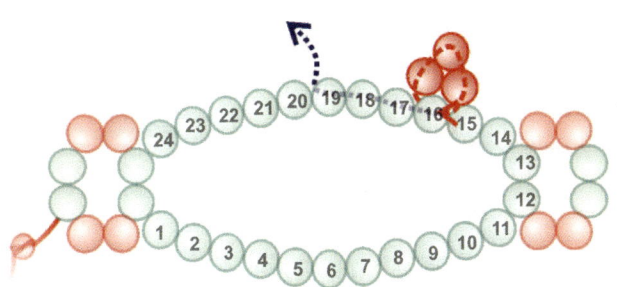

3. Pick up 2B, 2A, 2B, go with thread up through the 12th through 16th A beads added in step #2.

4. Pick up 3B, go with thread right to left through the 16th through 19th A beads, step #2.

sky blue aqua bracelet 11

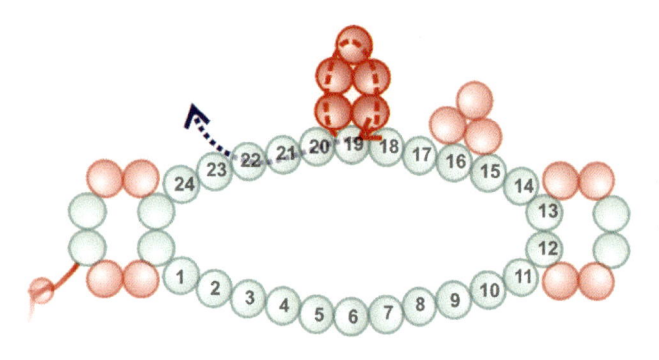

5. Pick up 5B, go with thread right to left through the 19th through 22nd A beads added in step #2.

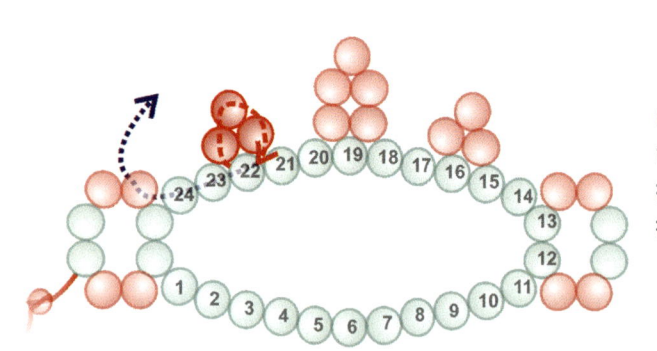

6. Pick up 3B, go with thread right to left through the 22nd through 24th A beads, step #2 and the 2nd B bead, step #1, (FT) or step #3, (ETA).

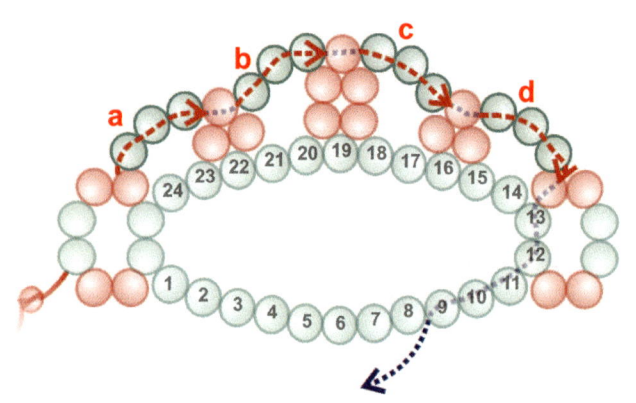

7. a) Pick up 3A, go with thread left to right through the 2nd B bead, step #6.
b) Pick up 3A, go with thread left to right through the 3rd B bead, step #5.
c) Pick up 3A, go with thread left to right through the 2nd B bead, step #4.
d) Pick up 3A, go with thread right to left through the 1st B bead added in step #3 and down through the 13th through 9th A beads added in step #2.

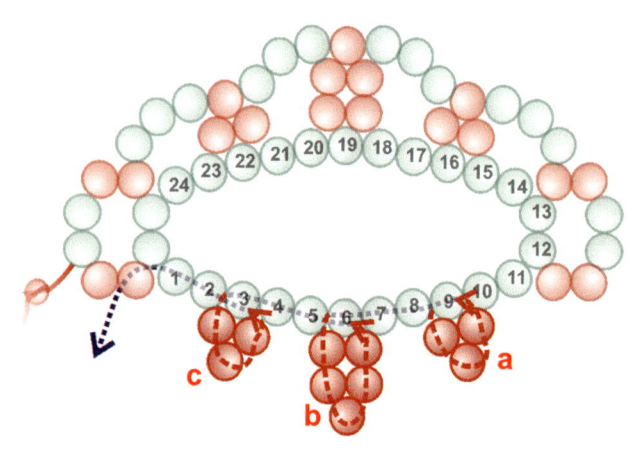

8. a) Pick up 3B, go with thread right to left through the 9th through 6th A beads, step #2.
b) Pick up 5B, go with thread right to left through the 6th through 3rd A beads, step #2.
c) Pick up 3B, go with thread right to left through the 3rd through 1st A bead, step #2 and the 1st B bead (of the 2nd set of 2B) added in step #1 (FT) or step #3 (ETA).

12 beaded bracelets pattern collection

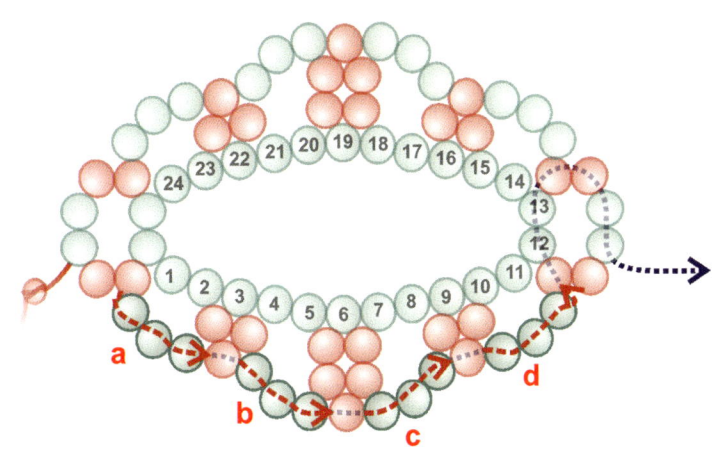

9. a) Pick up 3A, go with thread left to right through the 2nd B bead, step #8c.
b) Pick up 3A, go with thread left to right through the 3rd B bead, step #8b.
c) Pick up 3A, go with thread left to right through the 2nd B bead, step #8a.
d) Pick up 3A, go with thread right to left through the 2nd B bead (of the 2nd set of 2B) added in step #3, up through the 12th and 13th A beads, step #2, left to right the 1st set of 2 B beads, #3 and down through the 2 A beads, #3.

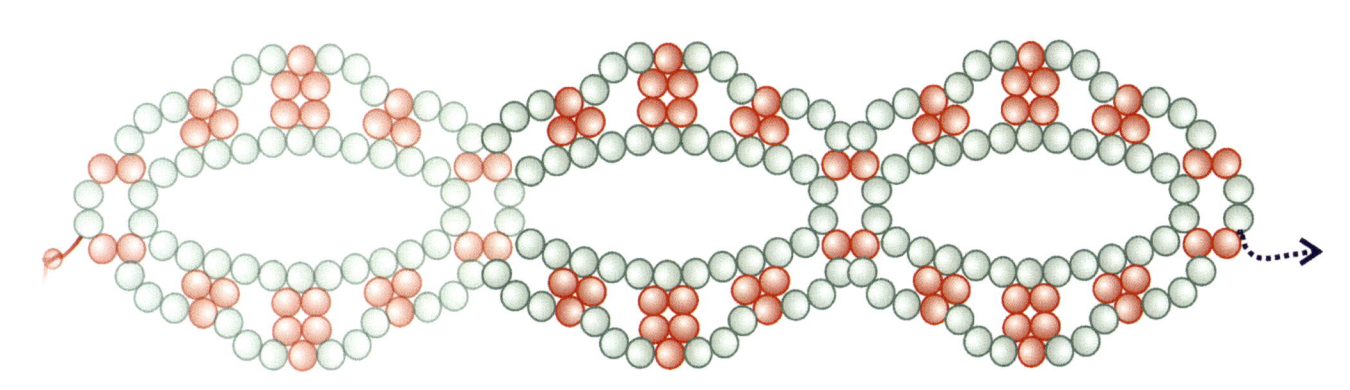

10. Continue bracelet by repeating steps #2 through #9, until it fits.

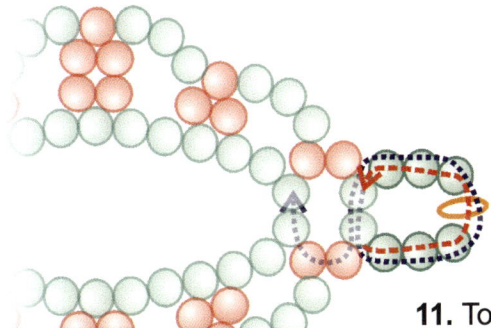

11. To add clasp, pick up 3A, clasp, 3A, go with thread down through 2 A beads in bracelet. Continue with working thread around through the clasp beads several times. Weave the working thread into the bracelet and end. Repeat the clasp directions in the same manner on the other end after removing the stopper bead.

sky blue aqua bracelet

Gold Time Bracelet

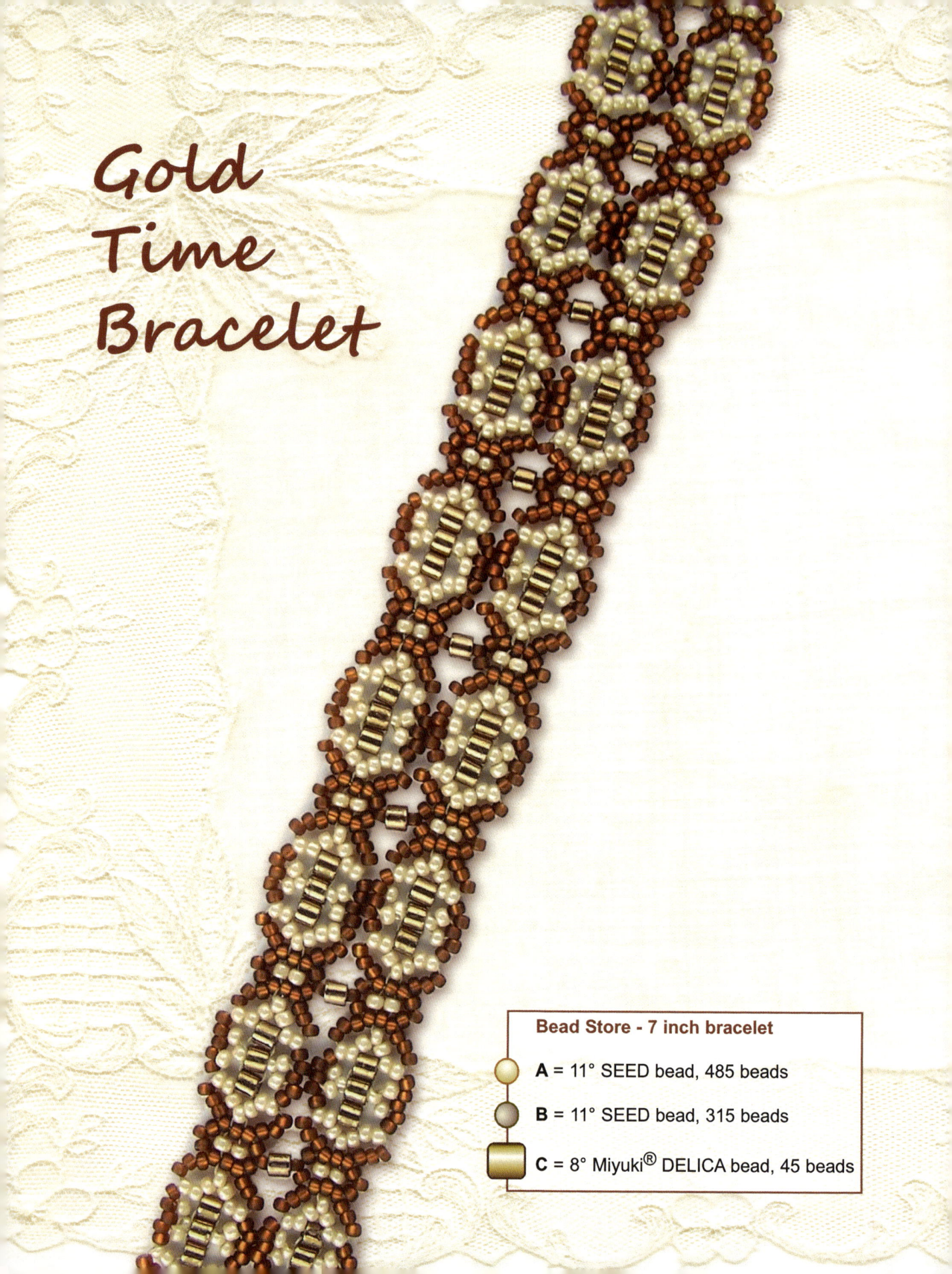

Bead Store - 7 inch bracelet

A = 11° SEED bead, 485 beads

B = 11° SEED bead, 315 beads

C = 8° Miyuki® DELICA bead, 45 beads

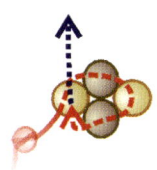

1. Pick up 1A, 1B, 1A, 1B, go with thread forward through the 1st A bead just added.

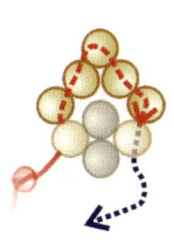

2. Pick up 5A, go with thread down through the 2nd A bead added in step #1.

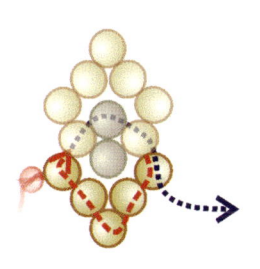

3. Pick up 5A, go with thread forward through the 1st A, 1st B, 2nd A bead added in step #1 and the 1st A bead just added in this step.

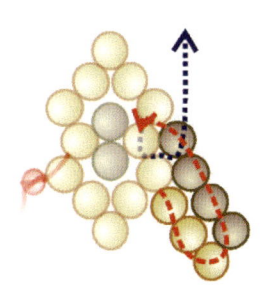

4. Pick up 3A, 4B, go with thread down through the 2nd A bead added in step #1 or the 1st A bead step #14 and up through the 4th B bead just added in this step.

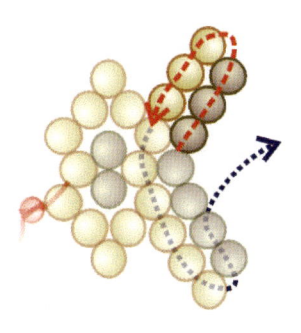

5. Pick up 3B, 3A, go with thread down through the 5th A bead, step #2 or the 4th A bead step #16, the 2nd A bead, step #1 or the 1st A bead step #14, the 1st A bead, step #3 or #15, down through the 1st, 2nd, and 3rd A beads, step #4, and up through the 1st and 2nd B beads, step #4.

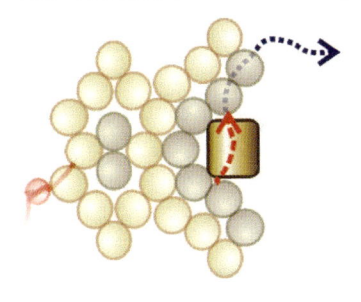

6. Pick up 1C, go with thread up through the 2nd and 3rd B beads, step #5.

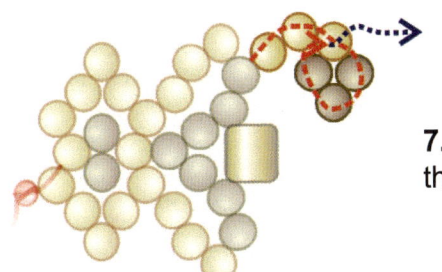

7. Pick up 3A, 3B, go with thread forward through the 3rd A bead, just added in this step.

gold time bracelet pattern 15

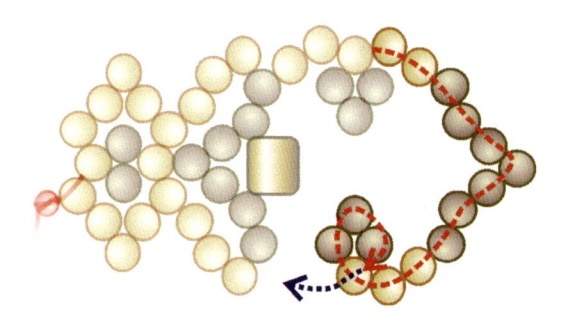

8. Pick up 2A, 7B, 3A, 3B, go with thread forward through the 3rd A bead just added in this step.

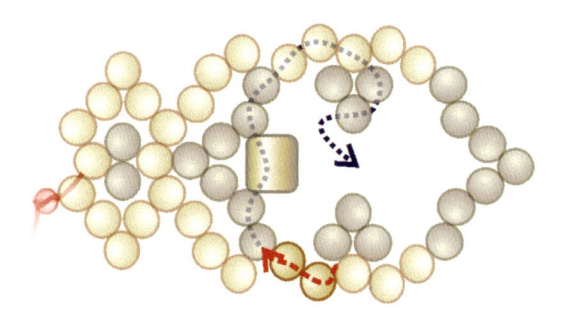

9. Pick up 2A, go with thread up through the 1st and 2nd B beads, step #4, the C bead, the 2nd and 3rd B beads, step #5, forward through 3 A and the 1st and 2nd B beads added in step #7.

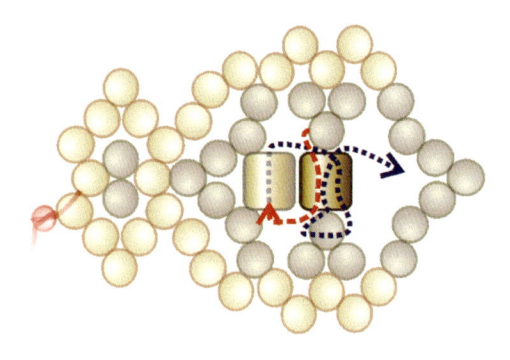

10. Pick up 1C, go with thread up through the C bead added in step #6, down through the C bead just added in this step, the 2nd B bead (of the 3B), step #8 and up through the C bead added in this step.

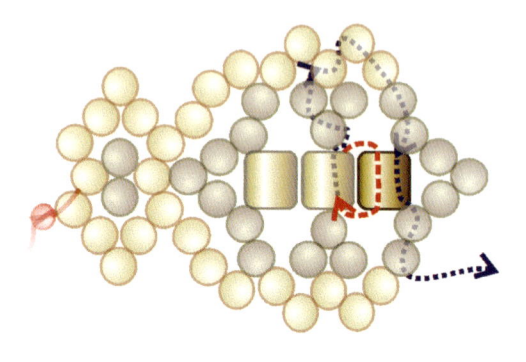

11. Pick up 1C, go with thread up through the C bead added in step #10, forward through the 2nd and 3rd B beads, the 3rd A bead, step #7, 2 A and 1st and 2nd B beads, step #8, the C bead just added in this step and down through the 6th and 7th B beads, step #8.

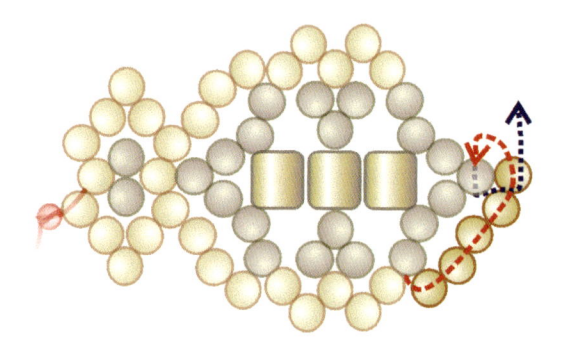

12. Pick up 5A, go with thread down through the 4th B bead added in step #8, and up through the 5A bead just added in this step.

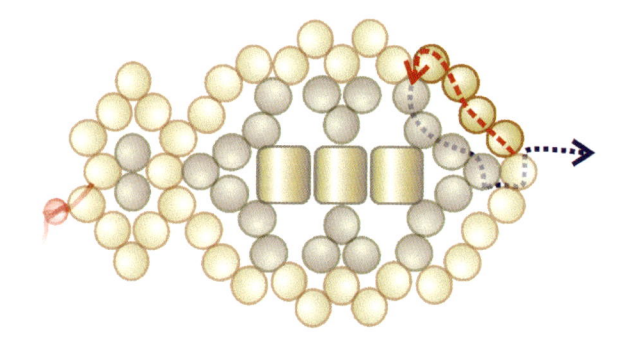

13. Pick up 4A, go with thread down through the 1st, 2nd, 3rd and 4th B beads, step #8 and up through the 5th A bead, step #12.

16 beaded bracelets pattern collection

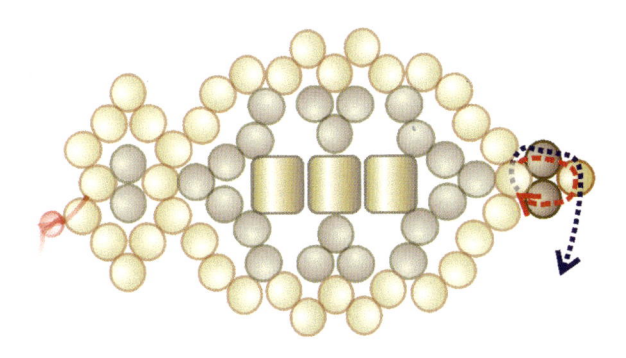

14. Pick up 1B, 1A, 1B, go with thread up through the 5th A bead, step #12 and forward through the 1st B and A beads just added in this step.

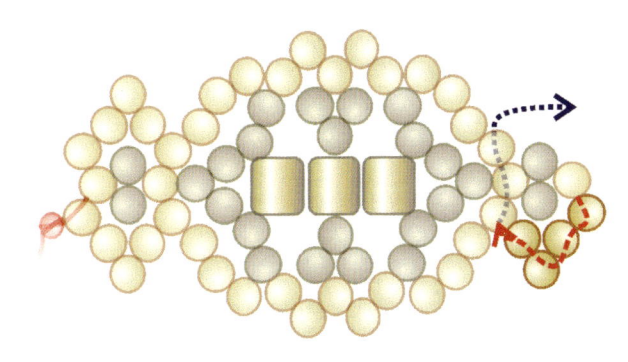

15. Pick up 4A, go with thread up through the 4th and 5th A beads, step #12 and the 1st A bead, step #13.

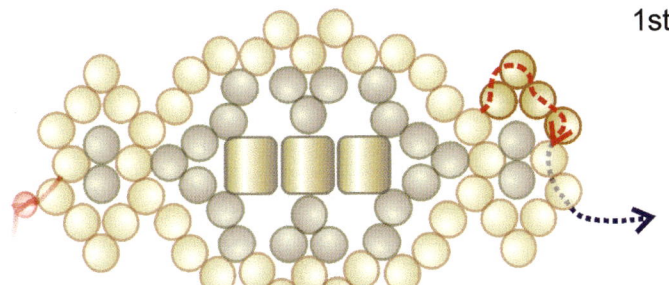

17. Continue bracelet by repeating steps #4 through #16, until the bracelet fits.

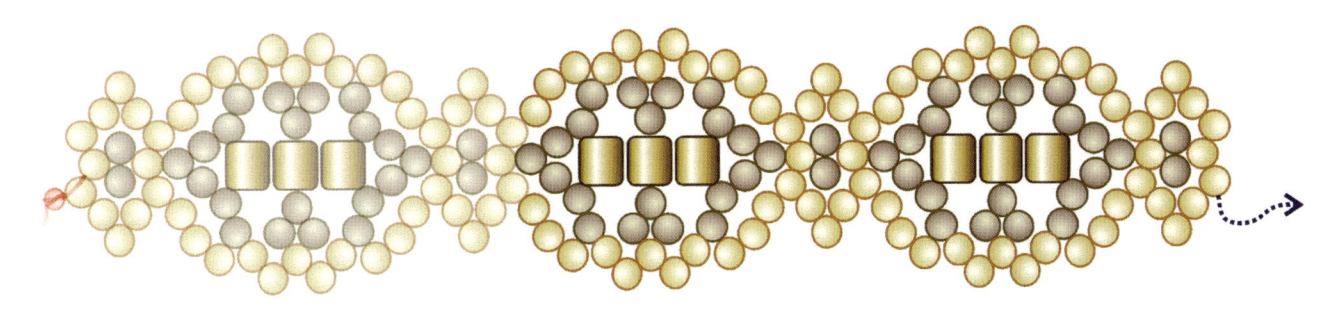

16. Pick up 4A, go with thread down through the 1 A bead added in step #14 and the 1st A bead added in step #15.

gold time bracelet pattern 17

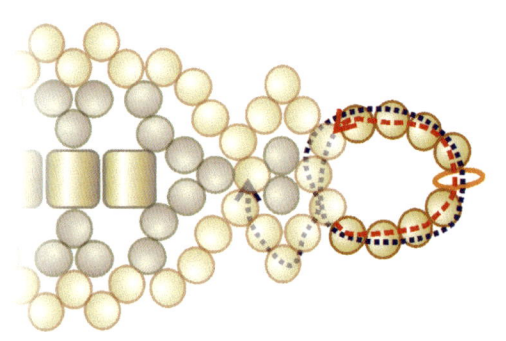

If you would like to do only one row for your bracelet, add clasp here. If you would like to do the double wide bracelet, move onto step #19

18. To add clasp, pick up 4A, clasp, 4A, go with thread down through 3 center beads in bracelet. Continue with working thread around through the clasp beads several times. Weave the working thread into the bracelet and end. Repeat the clasp directions in the same manner on the other end after removing the stopper bead.

To make the double wide bracelet, set the first bracelet to the side and start a second bracelet

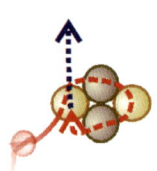

19. Pick up 1A, 1B, 1A, 1B, go with thread forward through the 1st A bead just added.

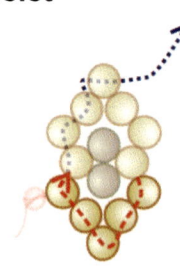

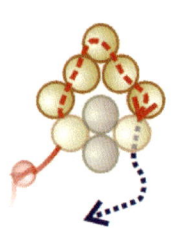

20. Pick up 5A, go with thread down through the 2nd A bead added in step #1.

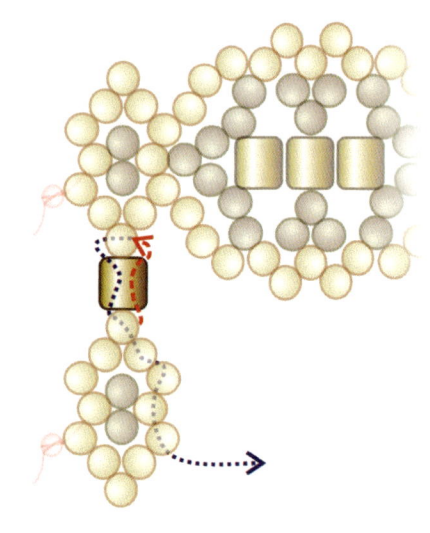

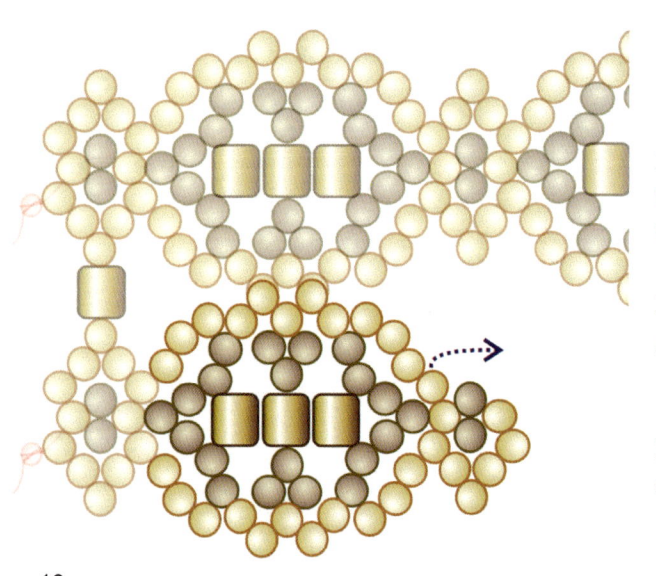

21. Pick up 5A, go with thread up through the 1st A, step #19, the 1st, 2nd and 3rd A beads, step #20.

22. Pick up 1C, go with thread right to left through the 3rd A bead, step #3 (added in the first row of bracelet), down through the 1 C bead just added, forward through the 3rd, 4th and 5th A beads, step #20, the 2nd A bead, step #19, and the 1st A bead, step #21.

23. Repeat steps #4 through #15 in the same manner.

18 beaded bracelets pattern collection

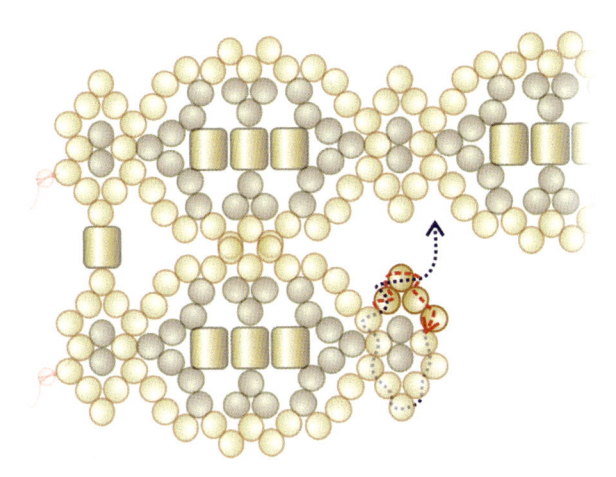

24. Pick up 4A, go with thread down through the 1 A bead, step #14 repeat, forward through the 4 A beads, step #15 repeat, up through the 4th and 5th A beads, step #12 repeat, the 1st A bead, step #13 repeat, the 1st and 2nd A beads just added in this step..

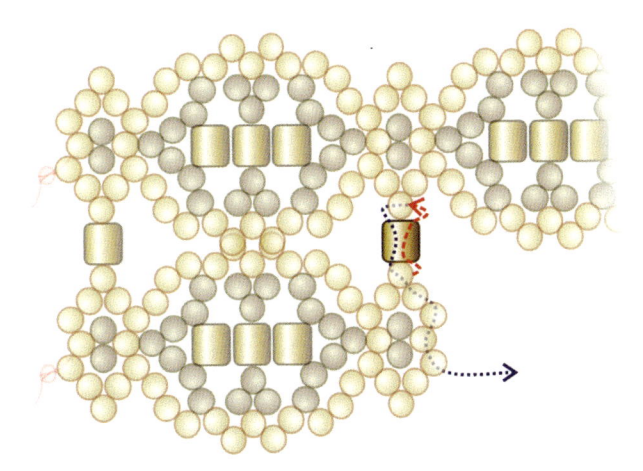

25. Pick up 1C, go with thread right to left through the 3rd A bead, step #15 (added in the first row of bracelet), down through the 1 C bead just added, forward through the 3rd, 4th and 5th A beads, step #24, the 2nd A bead, step #14 repeat, and the 1st A bead, step #15 repeat.

26. Continue second row of bracelet by repeating steps #23 through step #25 to the other end.

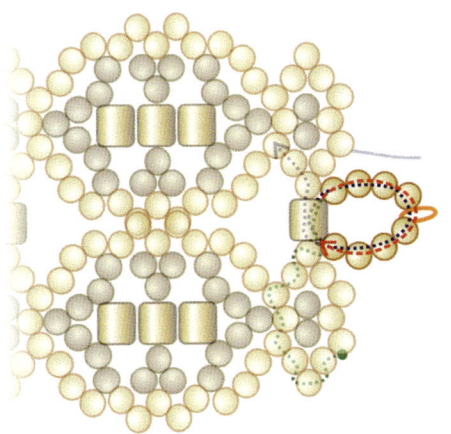

27. Go with working thread through the bracelet by following the green dotted line in illustration, coming out with thread up through the 1 C bead added in the last repeat of step #25. Pick up 4A, clasp, 4A, go with thread up through the 1 C bead in bracelet. Continue with working thread around through the clasp beads several times. Weave the working thread into the bracelet and end. Repeat the clasp directions in the same manner on the other end after removing the stopper bead.

gold time bracelet pattern 19

Aqua Lace Bracelet

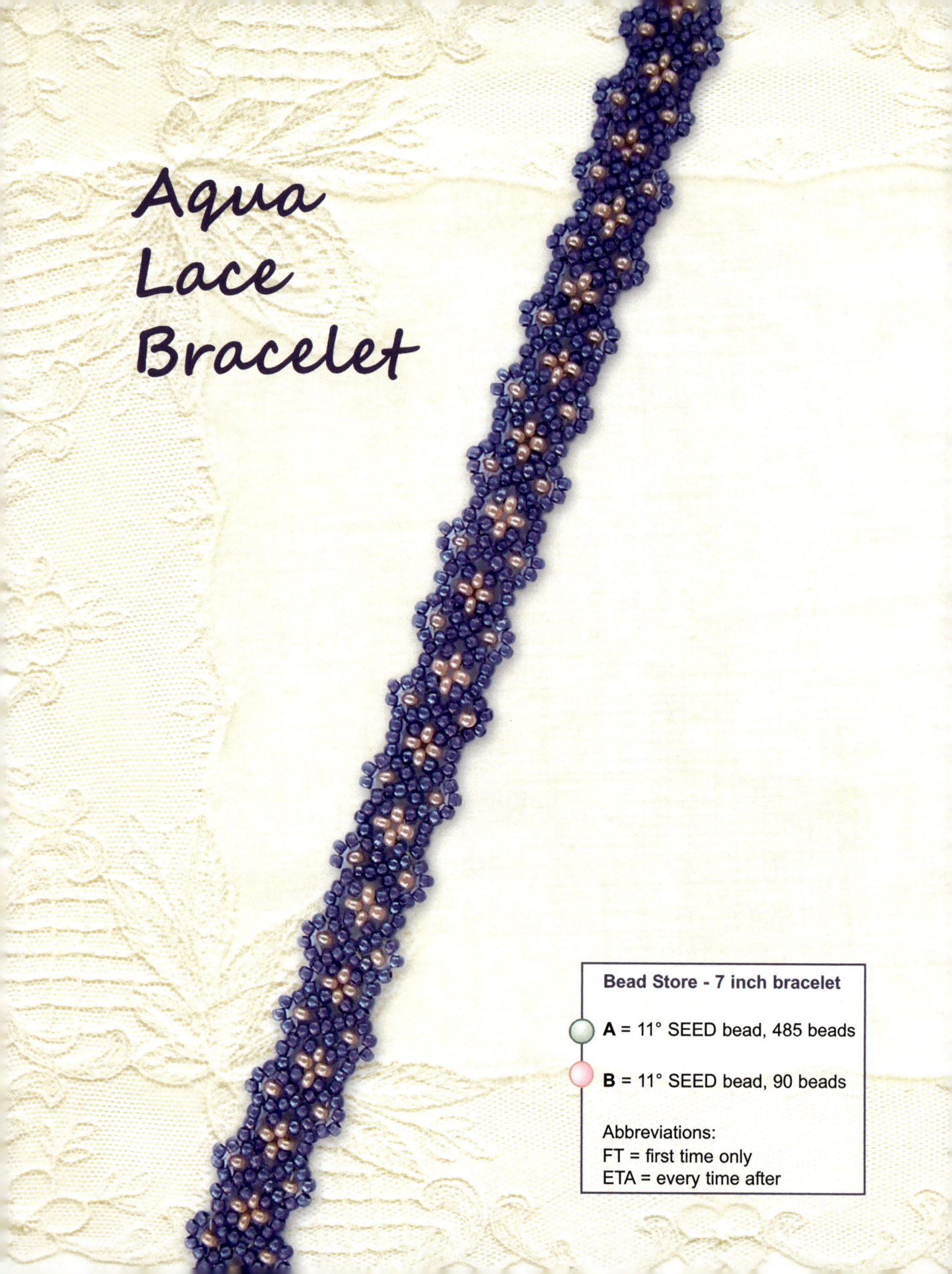

Bead Store - 7 inch bracelet

🟢 **A** = 11° SEED bead, 485 beads

🩷 **B** = 11° SEED bead, 90 beads

Abbreviations:
FT = first time only
ETA = every time after

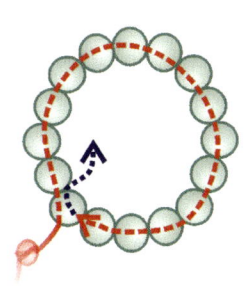

1. Pick up 16A, go with thread forward through the 1st A bead just added in this step.

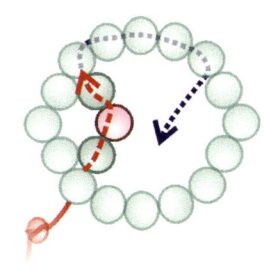

2. Pick up 1A, 1B, 1A, go with thread forward through the 5th through 9th A beads added in step #1.

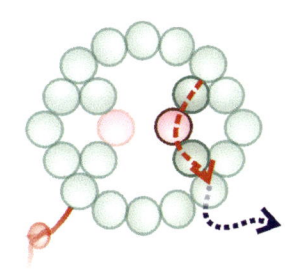

3. Pick up 1A, 1B, 1A, go with thread forward through the 13th A bead added in step #1.

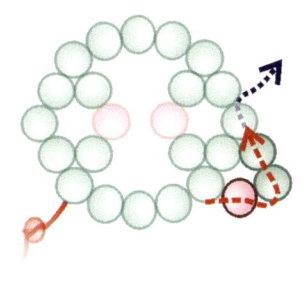

4. Pick up 1B, 2A, go with thread up through the 11th A bead added in step #1.

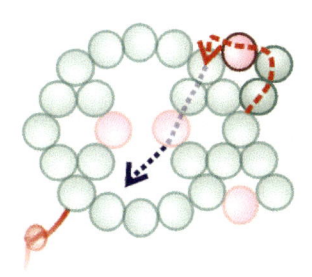

5. Pick up 2A, 1B, go with thread down through the 9th A bead, step #1, the 1st A and B beads added in step #3.

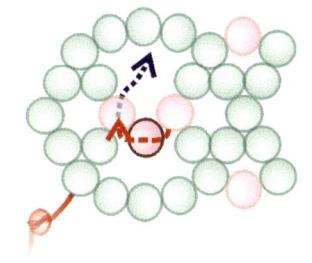

6. Pick up 1B, go with thread up through the B bead added in step #2.

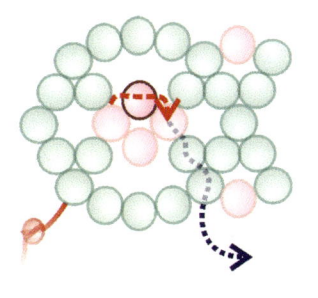

7. Pick up 1B, go with thread down through the B and 2nd A bead, step #3 and the 13th A bead, step #1.

aqua lace bracelet pattern 21

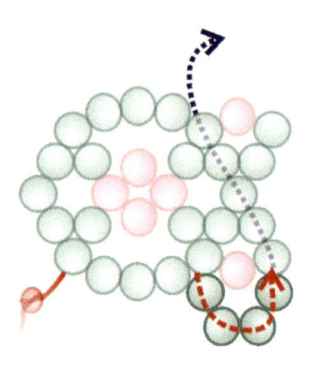

8. Pick up 4A, go with thread up through the 2 A beads, step #4, the 11th, 10th and 9th A beads added in step #1.

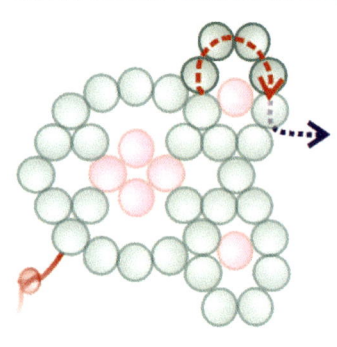

9. Pick up 4A, go with thread down through the 2nd A bead added in step #5.

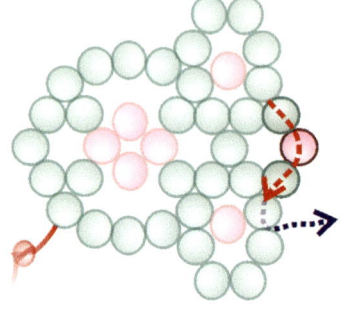

10. Pick up 1A, 1B, 1A, go with thread down through the 1st A bead added in step #4.

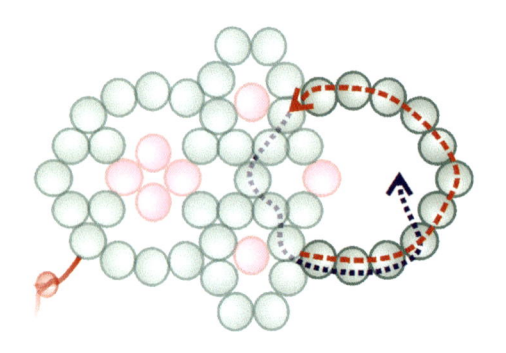

11. Pick up 11A, go with thread down through the 2 A beads, step #5 or #13a, the 11th A bead, step #1 (FT) or the 6th A bead, last repeat of step #11 (ETA) and the 2A beads, step #4 or #13b and the first 4 A beads just added in this step.

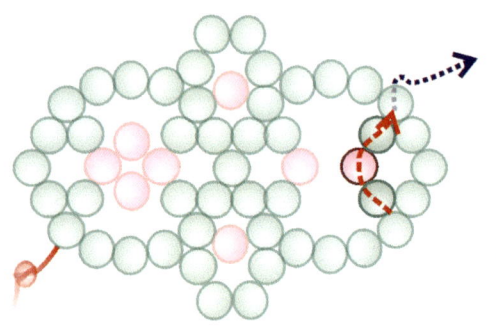

12. Pick up 1A, 1B, 1A, go with thread up through the 8th A bead added in step #11.

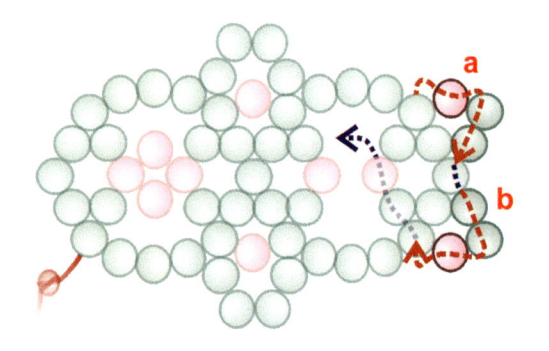

13. a) Pick up 1B, 2A, go with thread down through the 6th A bead, step #11.
b) Pick up 2A, 1B, go with thread up through the 4th A bead, step #11 and the 1st A and B beads, step #12.

22 beaded bracelets pattern collection

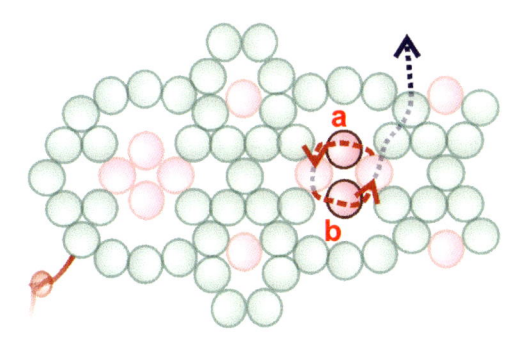

14. a) Pick up 1B, go with thread down through the B bead added in step #10 (first time), or step #16 (FT)
b) Pick up 1B, go with thread up through the B and 2nd A beads, step #12 and the 8th A bead, step #11.

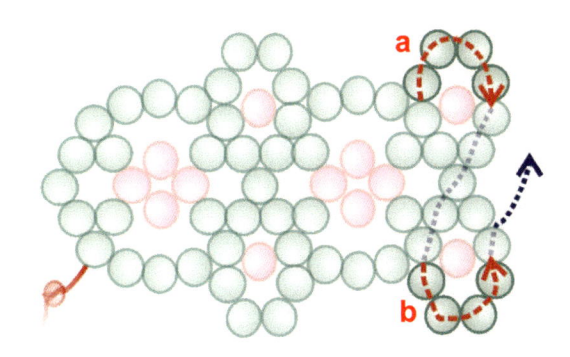

15. a) Pick up 4A, go with thread down through the 2 A beads, step #13a and the 6th, 5th and 4th A beads, step #11.
b) Pick up 4A, go with thread up through the 2nd A bead, step #13b.

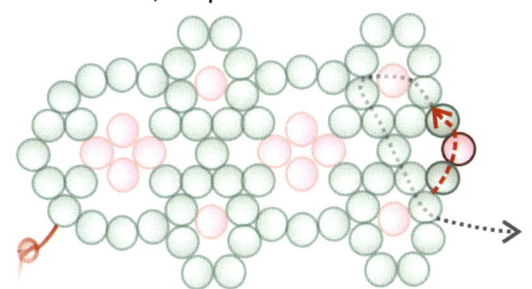

16. Pick up 1A, 1B, 1A, go with thread up through the 2nd A bead added in step #13a. Continue with working thread by following the blue dotted line in illustration, coming out with thread down through the 2nd A bead, step #13b.

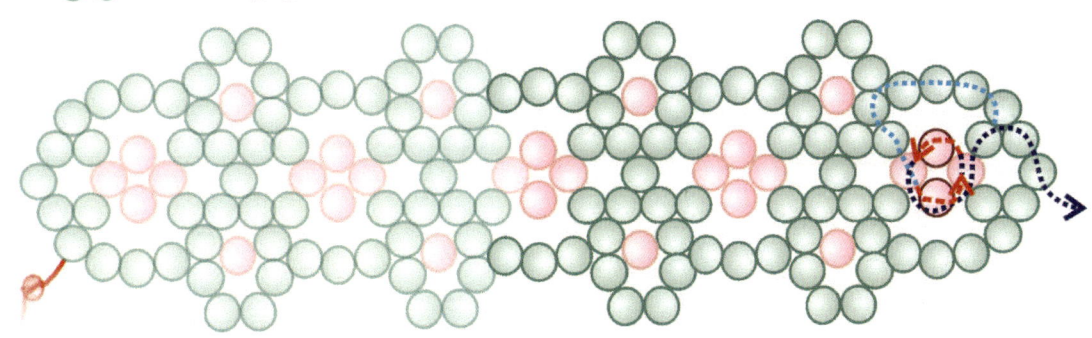

17. Continue bracelet by repeating steps #11 through #16 until the bracelet is about an inch from the length that you want your bracelet to be.
Repeat step #11, #12 and #14(a and b), skipping step #13.. Continue with working thread around, coming out at the 6th A bead added in the last repeat of step #11.

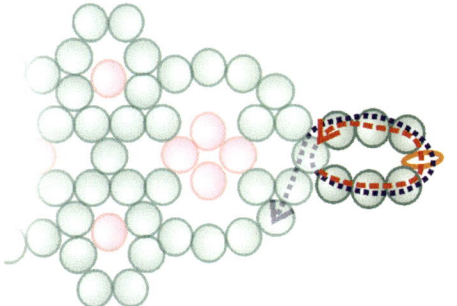

18. To add clasp, pick up 3A, clasp, 3A, go with thread down through 1 bead in bracelet. Continue with working thread around through the clasp beads several times. Weave the working thread into the bracelet and end. Repeat the clasp directions in the same manner on the other end after removing the stopper bead.

aqua lace bracelet pattern 23

Emerald Lace Bracelet

Bead Store - 7 inch bracelet

- **A** = 11° SEED bead, 520 beads
- **B** = 10° Miyuki® Triangle bead, 220 beads
- **C** = 8° Miyuki® DELICA bead, 60 beads

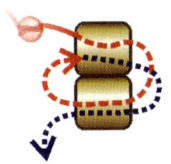

1. Pick up 2C, go with thread forward through both C beads again. Pull up thread and stack the beads as shown.

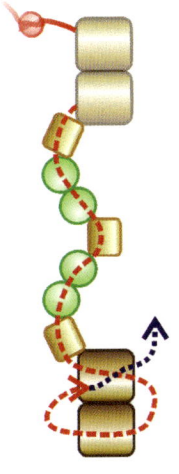

2. Pick up 1B, 2A, 1B, 2A, 1B, 2C, go with thread forward through the 1st C bead. Pull up thread and stack the C beads as shown.

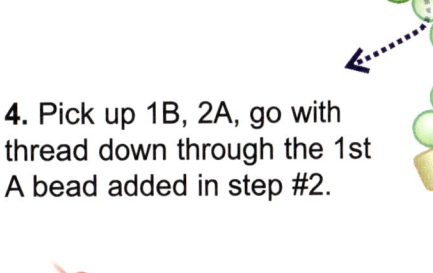

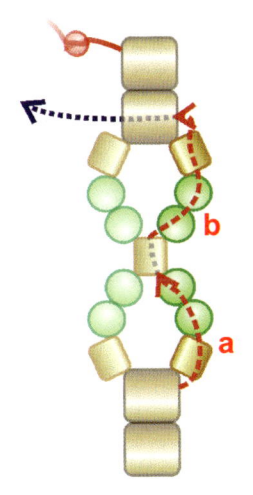

3. a) Pick up 1B, 2A, go with thread up through the 2nd B bead added in step #2.
b) Pick up 2A, 1B, go with thread right to left through the 2nd C bead added in step #1.

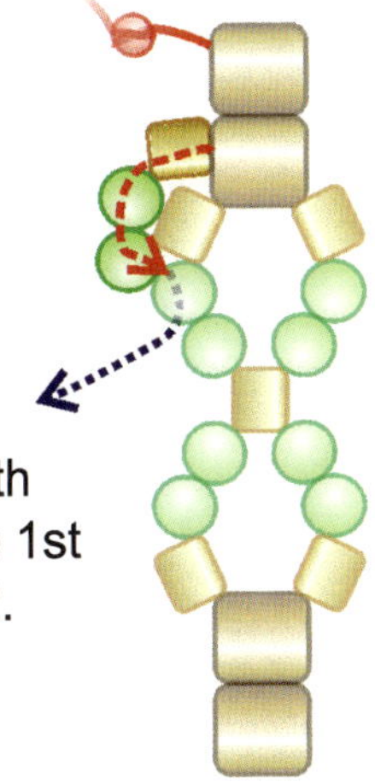

4. Pick up 1B, 2A, go with thread down through the 1st A bead added in step #2.

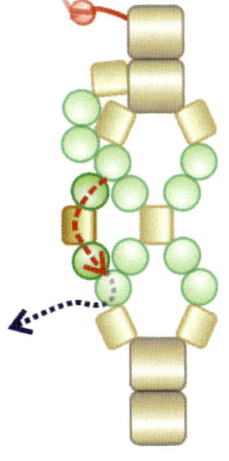

5. Pick up 1A, 1B, 1A, go with thread down through the last A bead added in step #2.

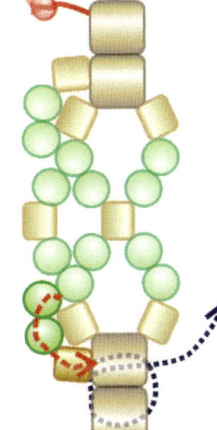

6. Pick up 2A, 1B, go with thread left to right through the 1st C bead, right to left through the 2nd C bead and left to right through the 1st C bead added in step #2.

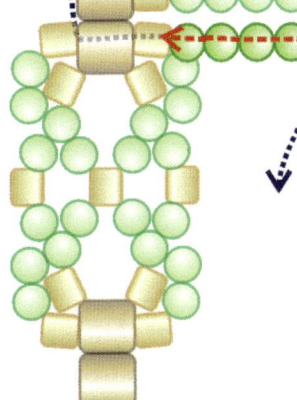

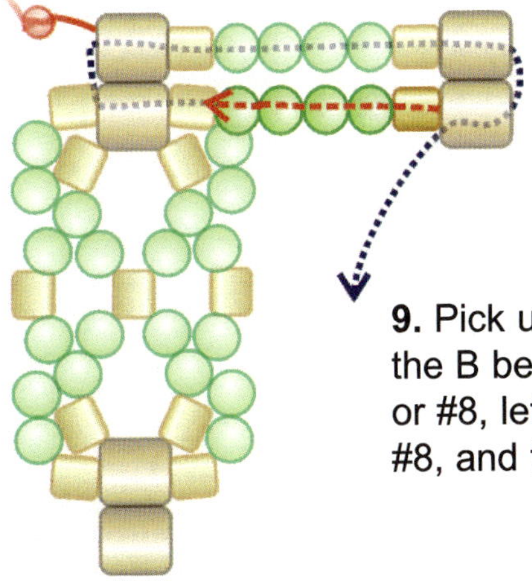

9. Pick up 1B, 4A, go with thread right to left through the B bead, step #7c or #15c, the 2nd C bead, step #1 or #8, left to right through the 1st C bead, step #1 or #8, and forward through all the beads added in step #8.

emerald lace bracelet pattern 25

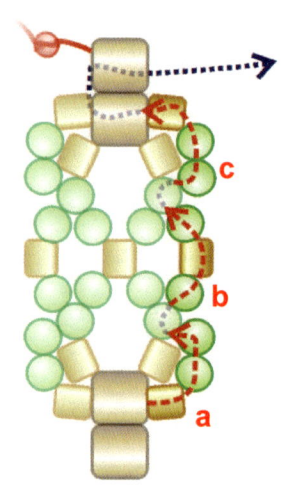

7. a) Pick up 1B, 2A, go with thread up through the 1st A bead, step #3a.
b) Pick up 1A, 1B, 1A, go with thread up through the 2nd A bead, step #3b.
c) Pick up 2A, 1B, go with thread right to left through the 2nd C bead and left to right through the 1st C bead, step #1.

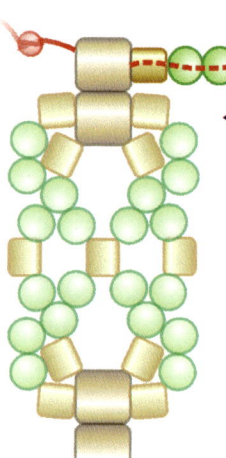

8. Pick up 1B, 4A, 1B, 2C, go with thread forward through the 2 C beads, pull up thread and stack the C beads as shown.

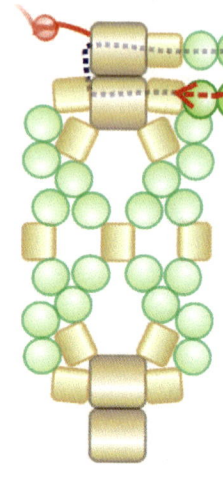

9. Pick up 1B, 4A, 2C, go with thread right to left through the 1 B bead, step #7c, 2nd C bead and left to right through the 1st C bead, step #1, and all the beads added in step #8.

10. Pick up 1B, 2A, 1B, 2A, 1B, 2C, go with thread forward through the 1st C bead and right to left through the 2nd C bead. Pull up thread and stack the C beads as shown.

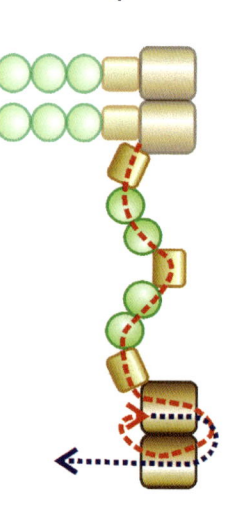

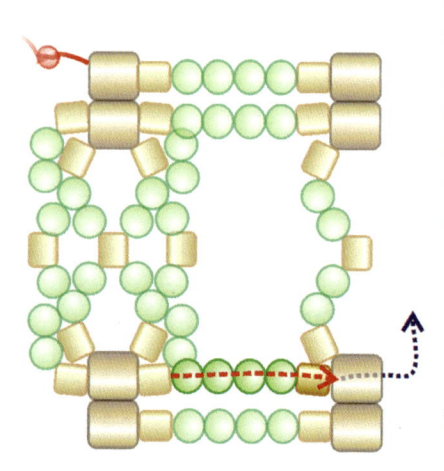

11. Pick up 1B, 4A, 1B, go with thread right to left through the 2nd C bead (step #2 or #10), left to right through the 1st C bead (step #2 or #10) and the 1st B bead (step #7a) or #15a.

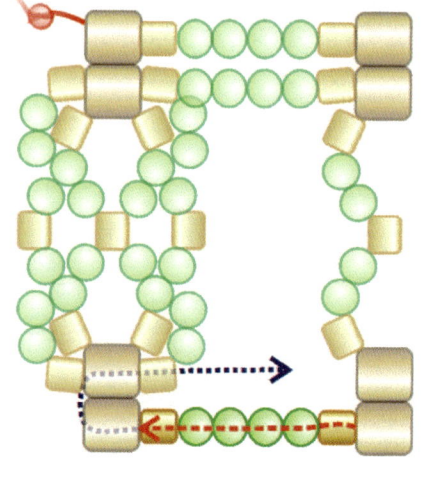

12. Pick up 4A, 1B, go with thread left to right through the 1st C bead, step #10.

26 beaded bracelets pattern collection

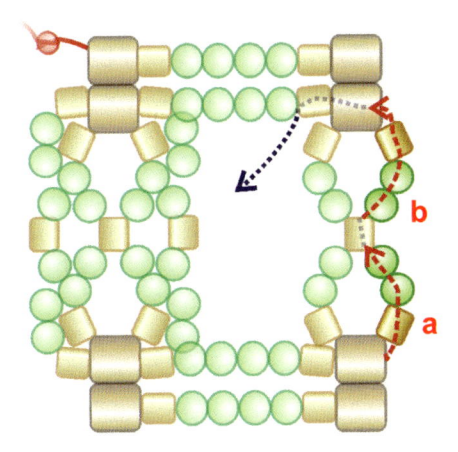

13. a) Pick up 1B, 2A, go with thread up through the 2nd B bead, step #10.
b) 2A, 1B, go with thread right to left through the 2nd C bead, step #8 and the B bead, step #9.

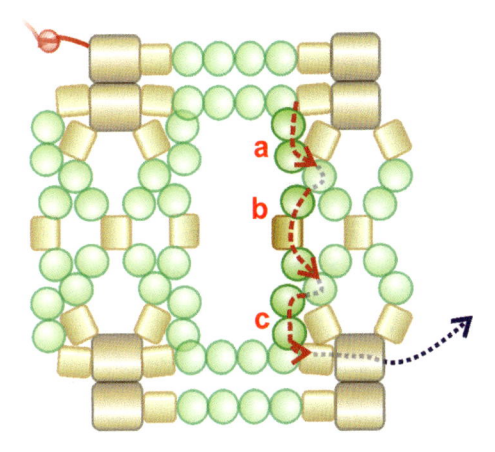

14. a) Pick up 2A, go with thread down through the 1st A bead, step #10.
b) Pick up 1A, 1B, 1A, go with thread down through the last A bead, step #10.
c) Pick up 2A, go with thread left to right through the B bead, step #12 and the 1st C bead, step #10.

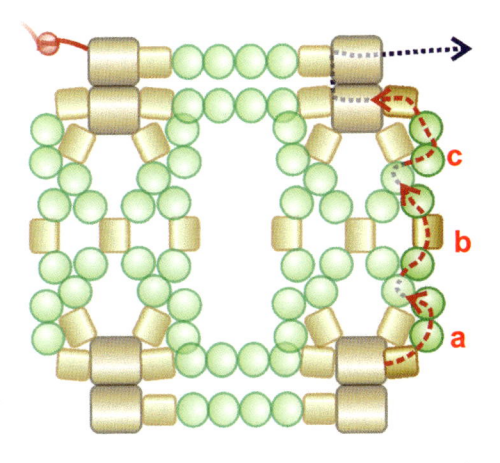

15. a) Pick up 1B, 2A, go with thread up through the 1st A bead, step #13a.
b) Pick up 1A, 1B, 1A, go with thread up through the 2nd A bead, step #13b.
c) Pick up 2A, 1B, go with thread right to left through the 2nd C bead and left to right through the 1st C bead, step #8.

16. Continue bracelet by repeating steps #8 through #15, until the bracelet fits.

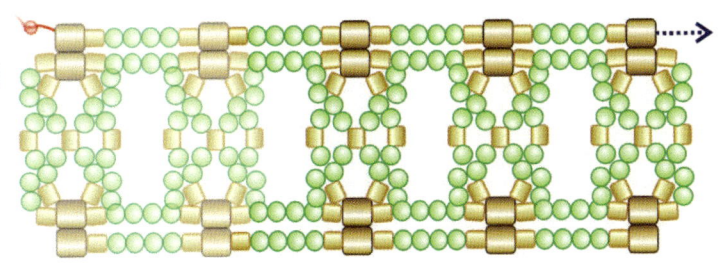

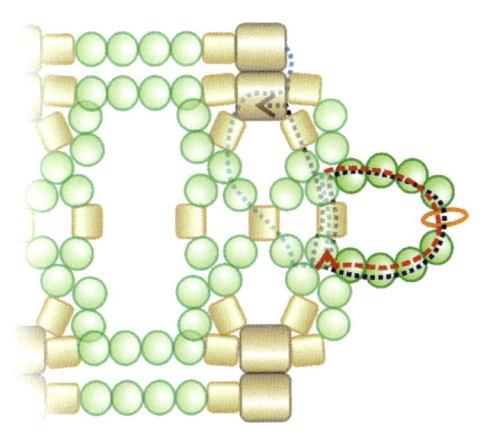

17. To add clasp, follow the blue dotted line in illustration, go with working thread down through the 2nd A bead, step #13a then up through the 1A, 1B and 1A beads, step #15b, pick up 4A, clasp, 4A, go with thread down through 3 center beads in bracelet. Continue with working thread around through the clasp beads several times. Weave the working thread into the bracelet and end. Repeat the clasp directions in the same manner on the other end after removing the stopper bead.

emerald lace bracelet pattern 27

Crystal Lace Bracelet

Bead Store - 7 inch bracelet

A = 11° SEED bead, 160 beads

B = 4mm Fire-polished crystal, 80 crystals

C = 4mm Crystal, 70 crystals

D = 8° Miyuki® DELICA bead, 10 beads

Abbreviations:
FT = first time only
ETA = every time after

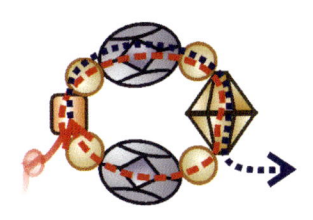

1. Pick up (1D, 1A, 1B, 1A, 1C), 1A, 1B, 1A, go with thread forward through the beads marked between () just added in this step.

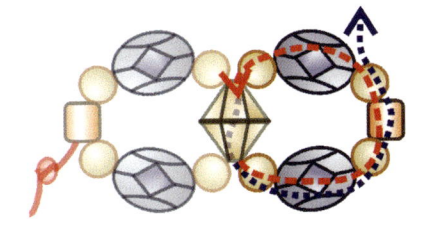

2. Pick up (1A, 1B, 1A, 1D, 1A), 1B, 1A, go with thread down through the C bead added in the last step (FT) or last repeat of step #5 (ETA) and forward through the beads marked between () just added in this step.

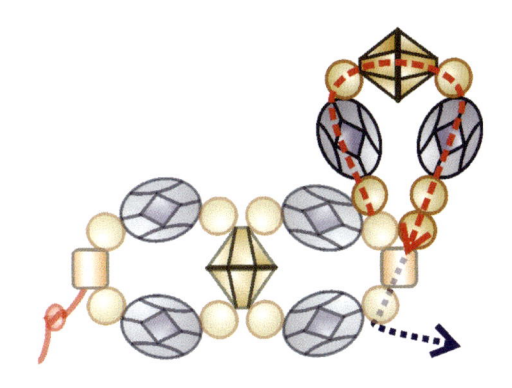

3. Pick up 1A, 1B, 1A, 1C, 1A, 1B, 2A, go with thread down through the 1 D and 1 A beads added in the last step.

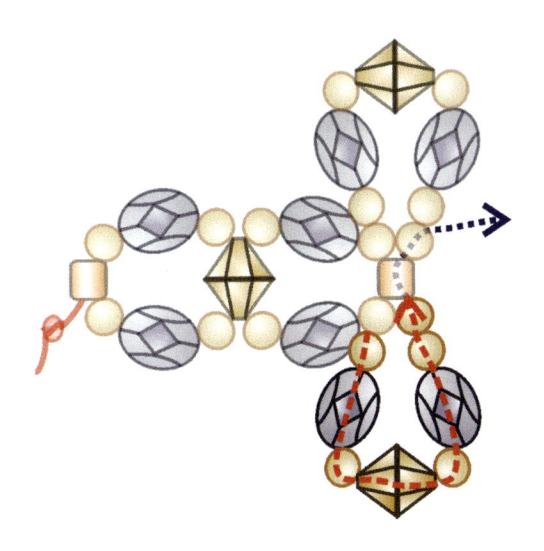

4. Pick up 1A, 1B, 1A, 1C, 1A, 1B, 2A, go with thread up through the 1 D bead, step #2 and the last A bead added in step #3.

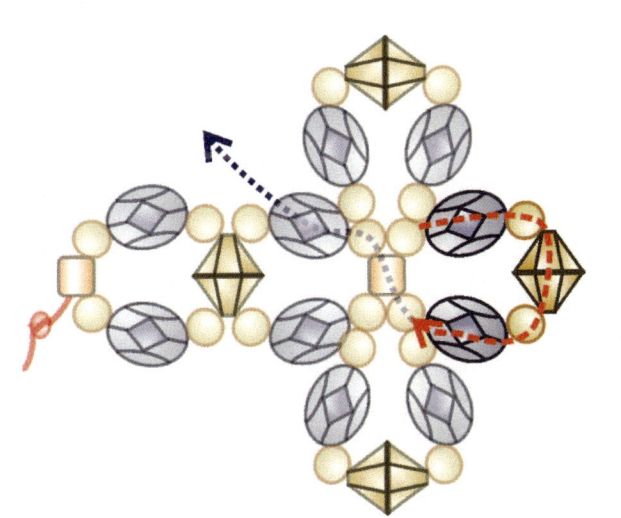

5. Pick up 1B, 1A, 1C, 1A, 1B, go with thread up through the last A bead, step #4, the D bead and the A and 2nd B beads added in step #2.

crystal lace bracelet pattern 29

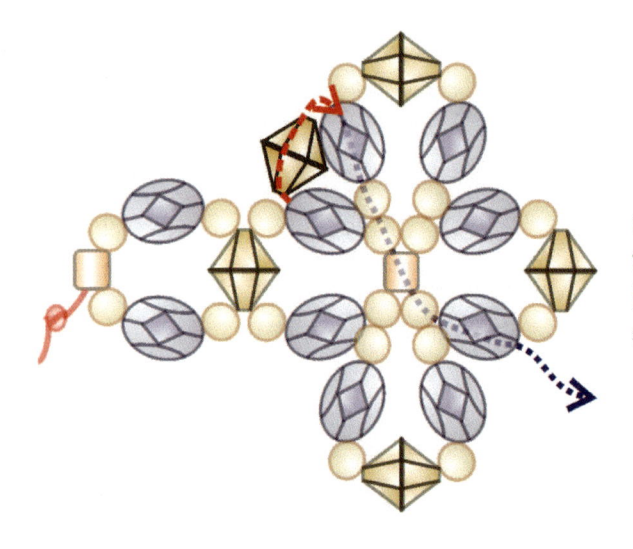

6. Pick up 1C, go with thread down through the 1st B and 1 A beads, step #3, the 3rd bead, the D bead, step #2, the last A bead, step #4 and the 2nd B bead, step #5.

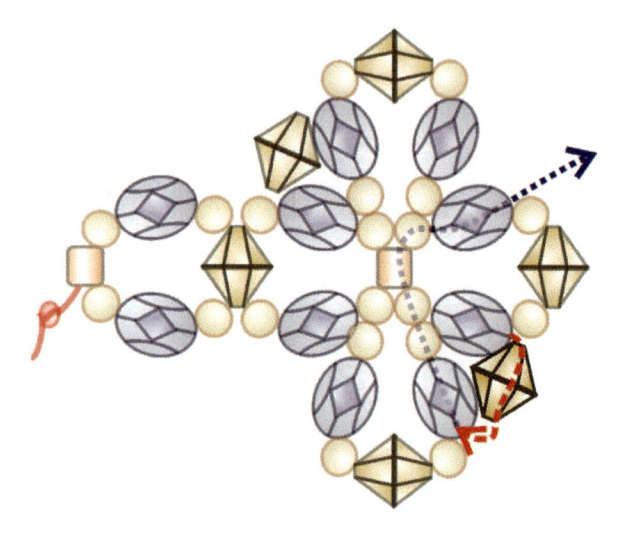

7. Pick up 1C, go with thread up through the 2nd B bead, 2 A beads, step #4, the D bead, step #2, the last A bead, step #3 and the 1st B bead, step #5.

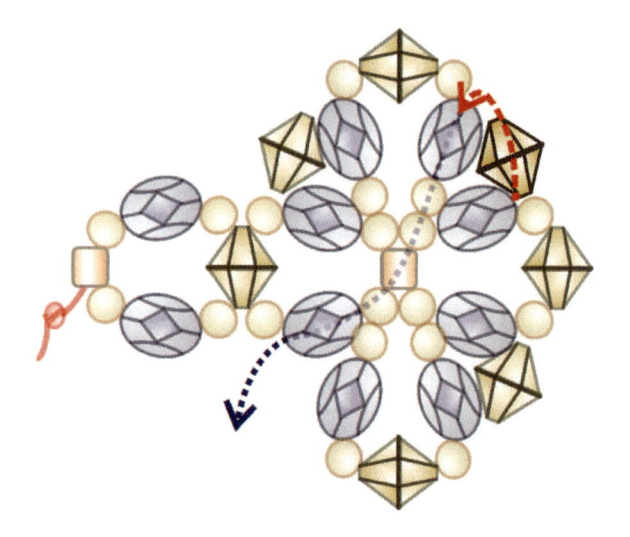

8. Pick up 1C, go with thread down through the 2nd B bead, 2 A beads, step #3, the D bead, 1 A bead and the 1st B bead, step #2.

30 beaded bracelets pattern collection

9. Pick up 1C, go with thread up through the 1st B and 1st A beads, step #4, the 2nd A bead, the D bead, step #2, the last A bead, step #3, the 1st B, A and C beads added in step #5.

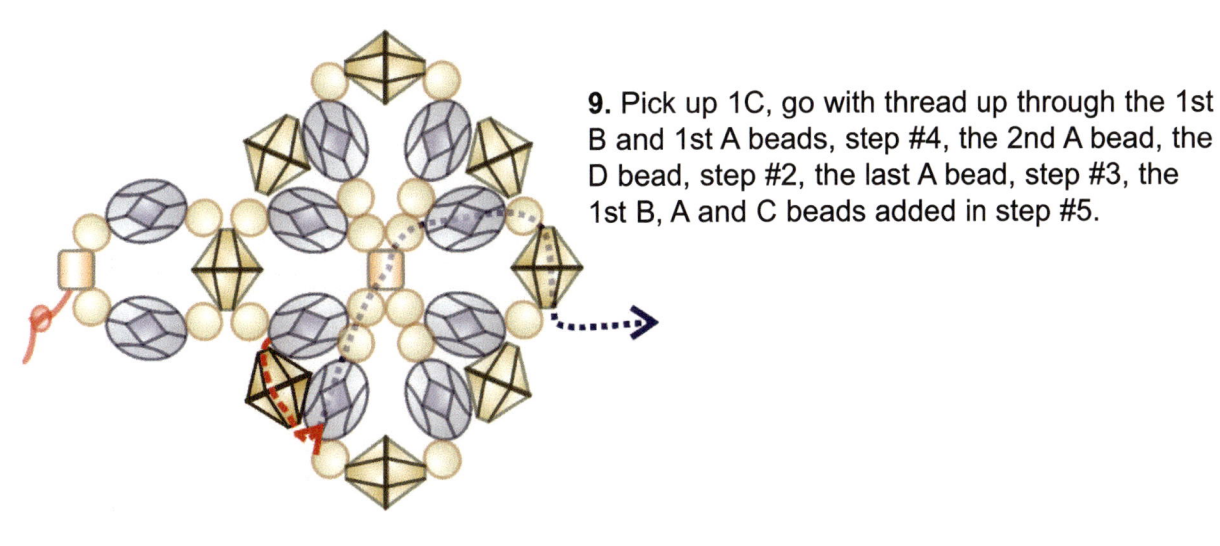

10. Continue bracelet by repeating steps #2 through #9, until the bracelet fits.

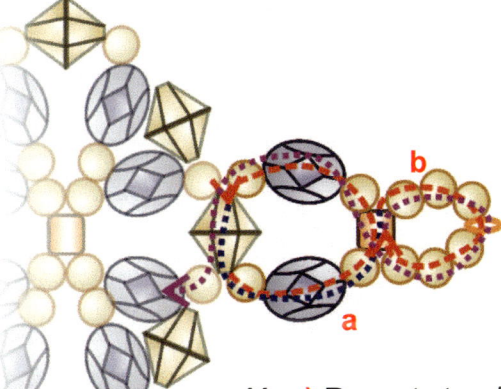

11. a) Repeat step #2, one time.
b) To add clasp, pick up 3A, clasp, 3A, go with thread down through 1 center bead in bracelet. Continue with working thread around through the clasp beads several times. Weave the working thread into the bracelet and end. Repeat the clasp (b) directions in the same manner on the other end after removing the stopper bead.

crystal lace bracelet pattern 31

Aqua Luster Bracelet

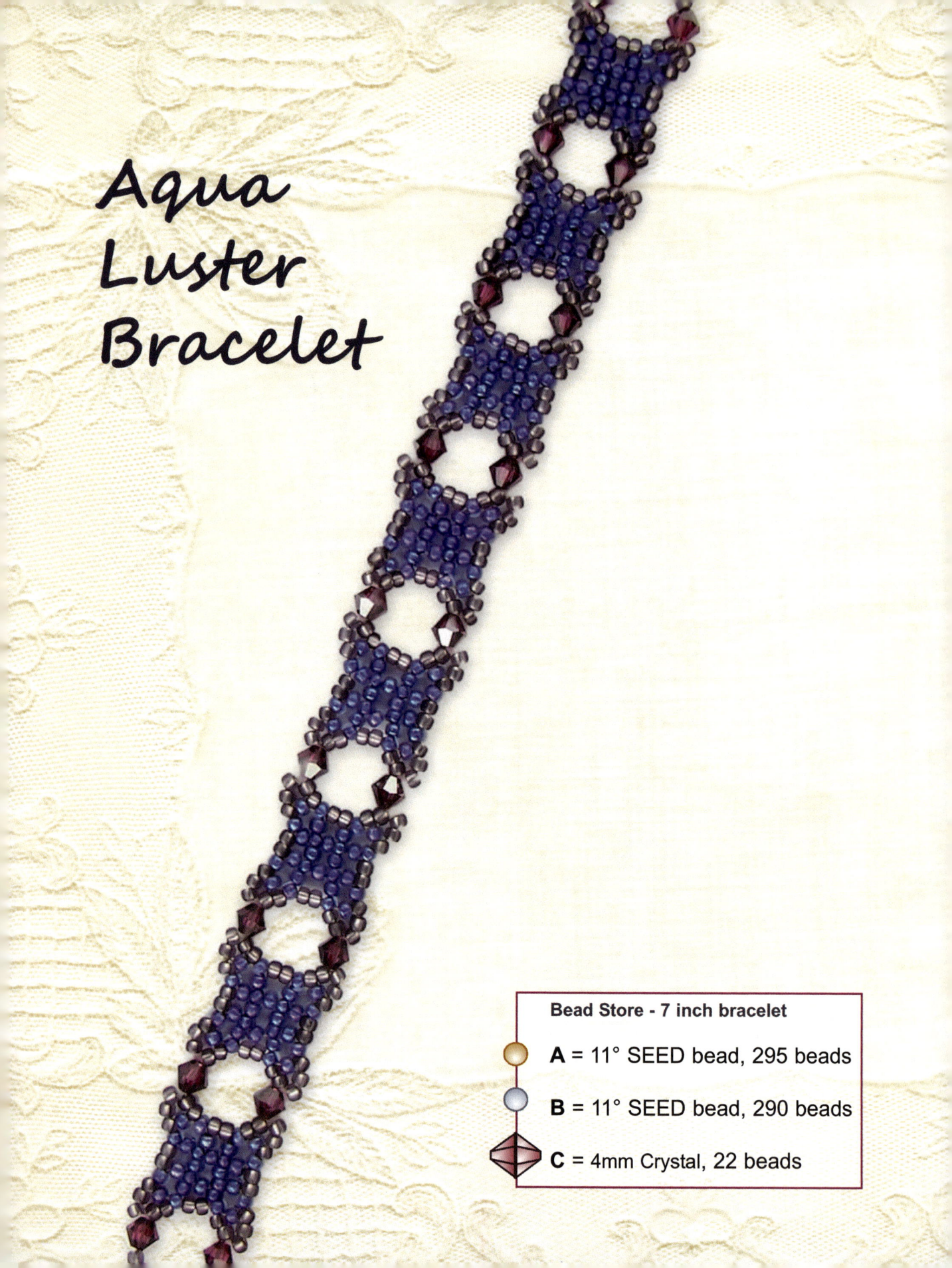

Bead Store - 7 inch bracelet

A = 11° SEED bead, 295 beads

B = 11° SEED bead, 290 beads

C = 4mm Crystal, 22 beads

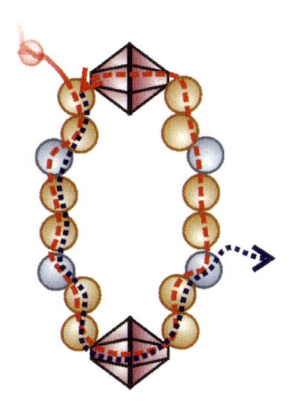

1. Pick up (2A, 1B, 2A, 1B, 2A, 1C, 2A, 1B), 2A, 1B, 2A, 1C, go with thread forward through the beads marked between ().

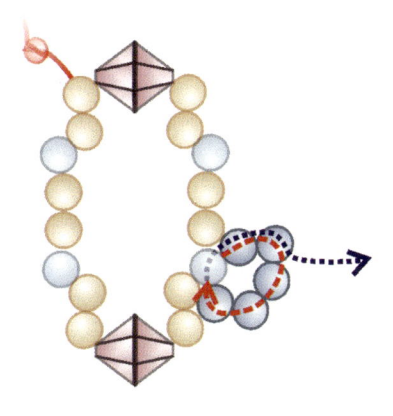

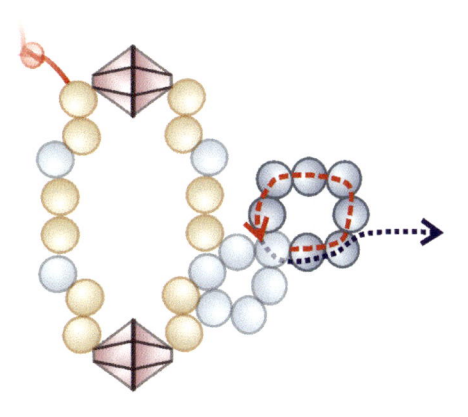

3. Pick up 7B, go with thread forward through the 2nd B bead added in the last step and the 1st and 2nd B beads, just added in this step.

2. Pick up 5B, go with thread up through the B bead added in the previous step and forward through the 1st and 2nd B beads, just added in this step.

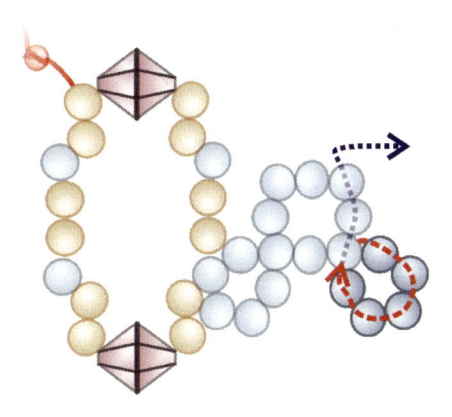

4. Pick up 5B, go with thread forward through the 2nd, 3rd and 4th B beads added in step #3.

aqua luster bracelet pattern 33

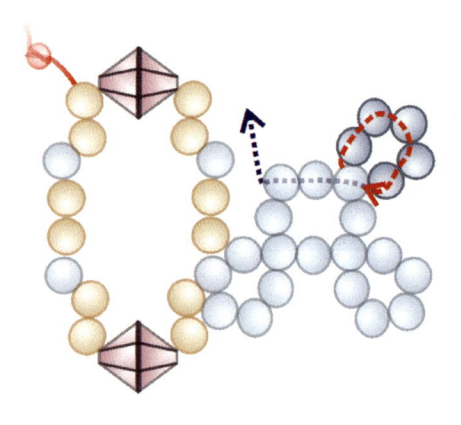

5. Pick up 5B, go with thread forward through the 4th, 5th and 6th B beads added in step #3.

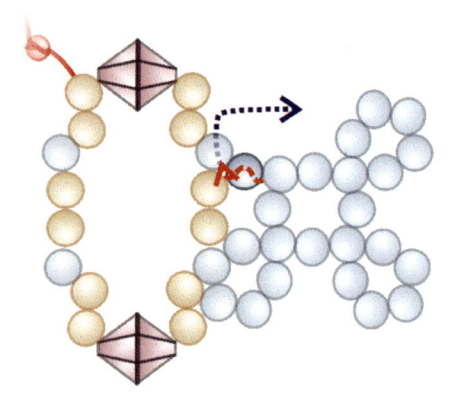

6. Pick up 1B, go with thread up through the 1 B bead added in step #1 or #18 as shown.

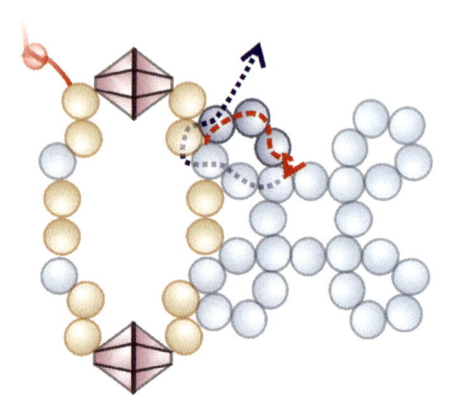

7. Pick up 3B, go with thread forward through the 6th B bead, step #3, 1 B, step #6, the 1 B and 1 A beads, step #1 or #18, as shown, and forward through the 1st B bead just added in this step.

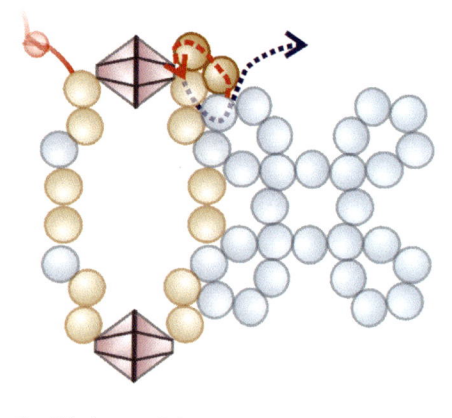

8. Pick up 2A, go with thread down through the top A bead (on the right side of top crystal), step #1 or #18 and forward through the 1st B bead added in step #7.

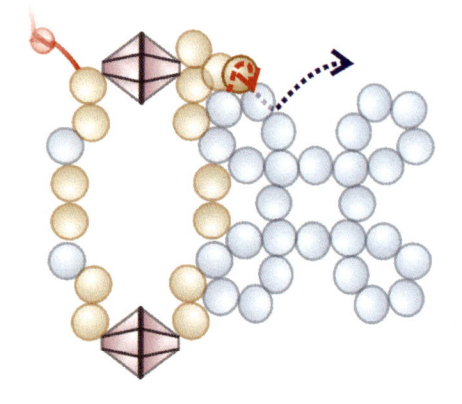

9. Pick up 1A, go with thread down through the 2nd B bead, step #7.

34 beaded bracelets pattern collection

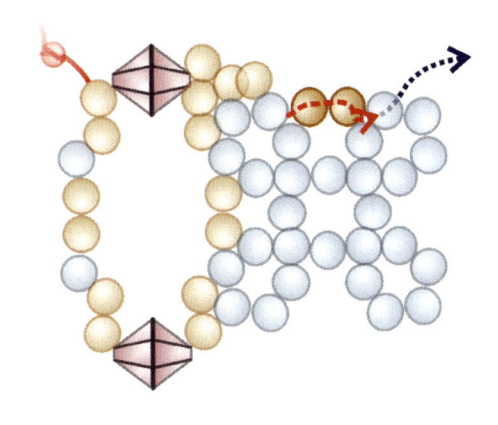

10. Pick up 2A, go with thread up through the 2nd B bead, step #5.

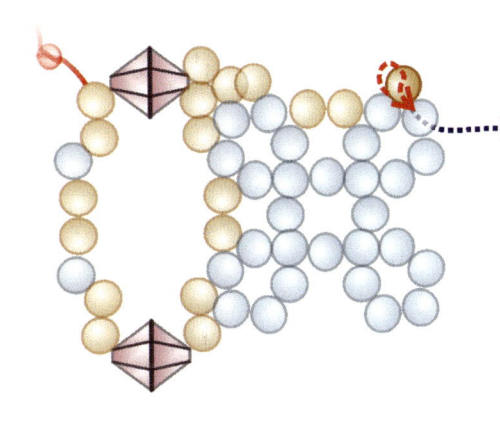

11. Pick up 1A, go with thread forward through the 3rd B bead, step #5.

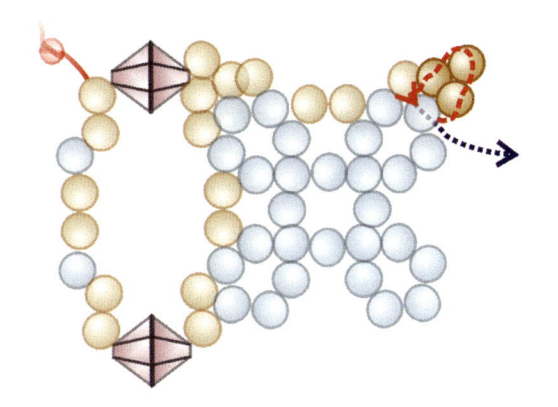

12. Pick up 3A, go with thread forward through the 3rd B bead, step #5.

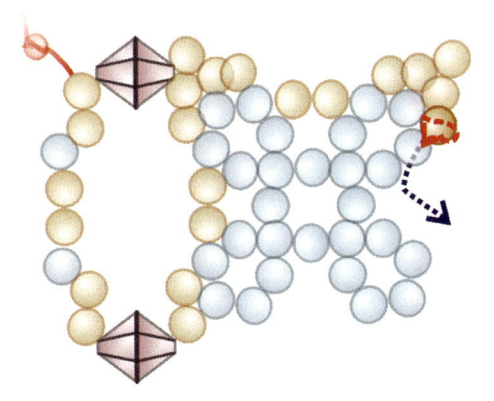

13. Pick up 1A, go with thread down through the 4th B bead, step #5.

aqua luster bracelet pattern 35

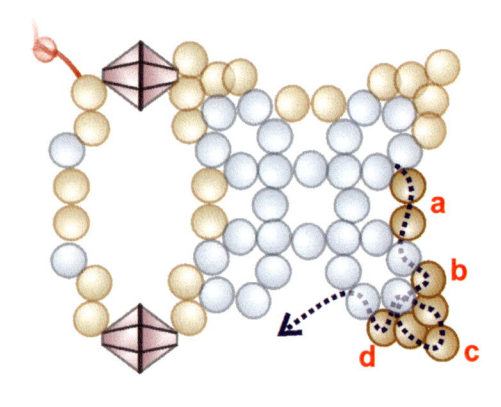

14. a) Pick up 2A, go with thread down through the 2nd B bead, step #4.
b) Pick up 1A, go with thread forward through the 3rd B bead, step #4.
c) Pick up 3A, go with thread forward through the 3rd B bead, step #4.
d) Pick up 1A, go with thread down (forward) through the 4th A bead, step #4.

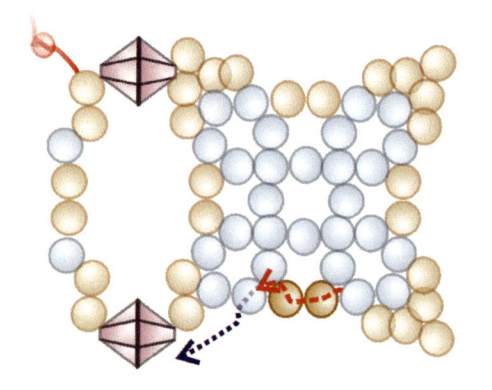

15. Pick up 2A, go with thread forward through the 4th A bead, step #2.

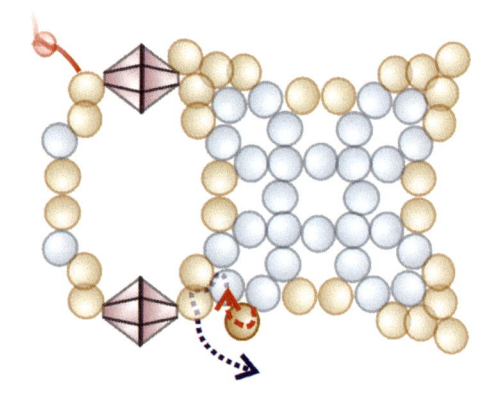

16. Pick up 1A, go with thread forward (up) through the 5th A bead, step #2 and down through the bottom A bead (on the right side of bottom crystal), step #1 or #18.

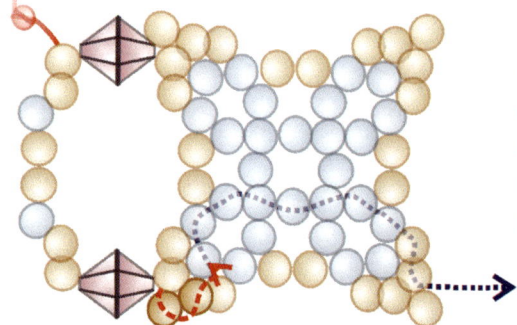

17. Pick up 2A, go with thread forward (up) through the 5th A bead, step #2. Continue with working thread through unit, coming out with thread down through the 3rd A bead, step #14c.

36 beaded bracelets pattern collection

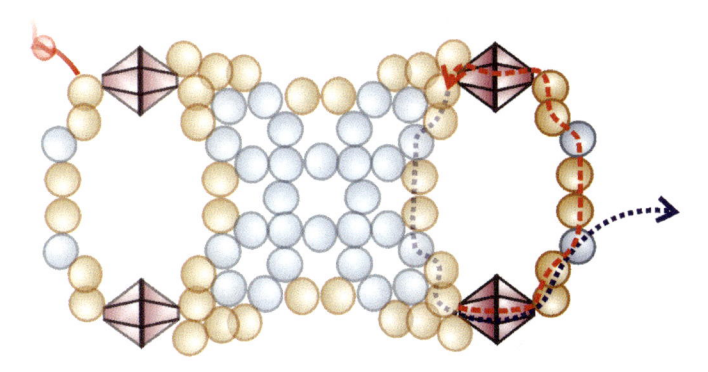

18. Pick up 1C, 2A, 1B, 2A, 1B, 2A, 1C, go with thread down through the 1st A bead, step #12, the A bead, step #13, the 4th B bead, step #5, 2 A beads, step #14a, the 2nd B bead, step #4, the A bead, step #14b and the 3rd A bead, step #14c, and forward through the 1C, 2A and 1B just added in this step.

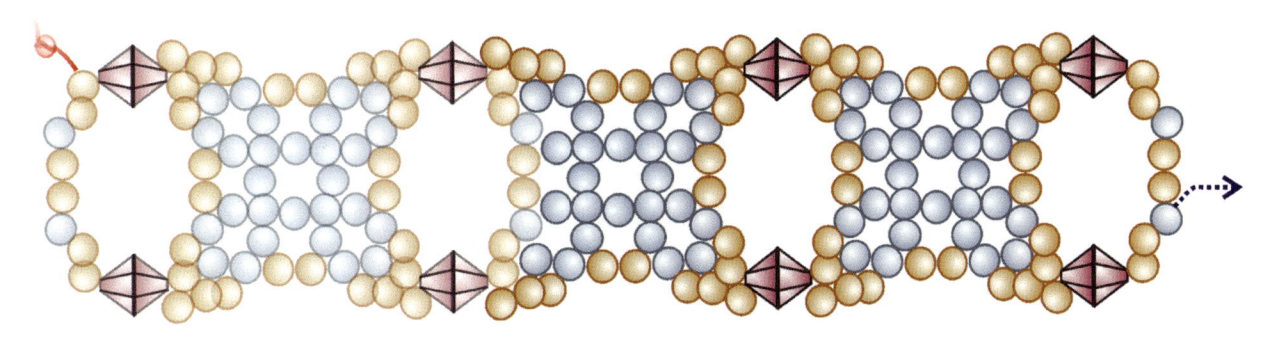

19. Continue bracelet by repeating steps #2 through #18 until the bracelet fits.

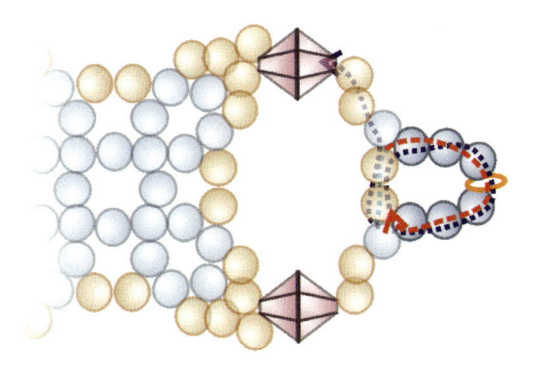

20. Go with working thread up through the 2 middle A beads added in the last repeat of step #18. To add clasp, pick up 3A, clasp, 3A, go with thread down through 2 beads in bracelet. Continue with working thread around through the clasp beads several times. Weave the working thread into the bracelet and end. Repeat the clasp directions in the same manner on the other end after removing the stopper bead.

Blue Lace Bracelet

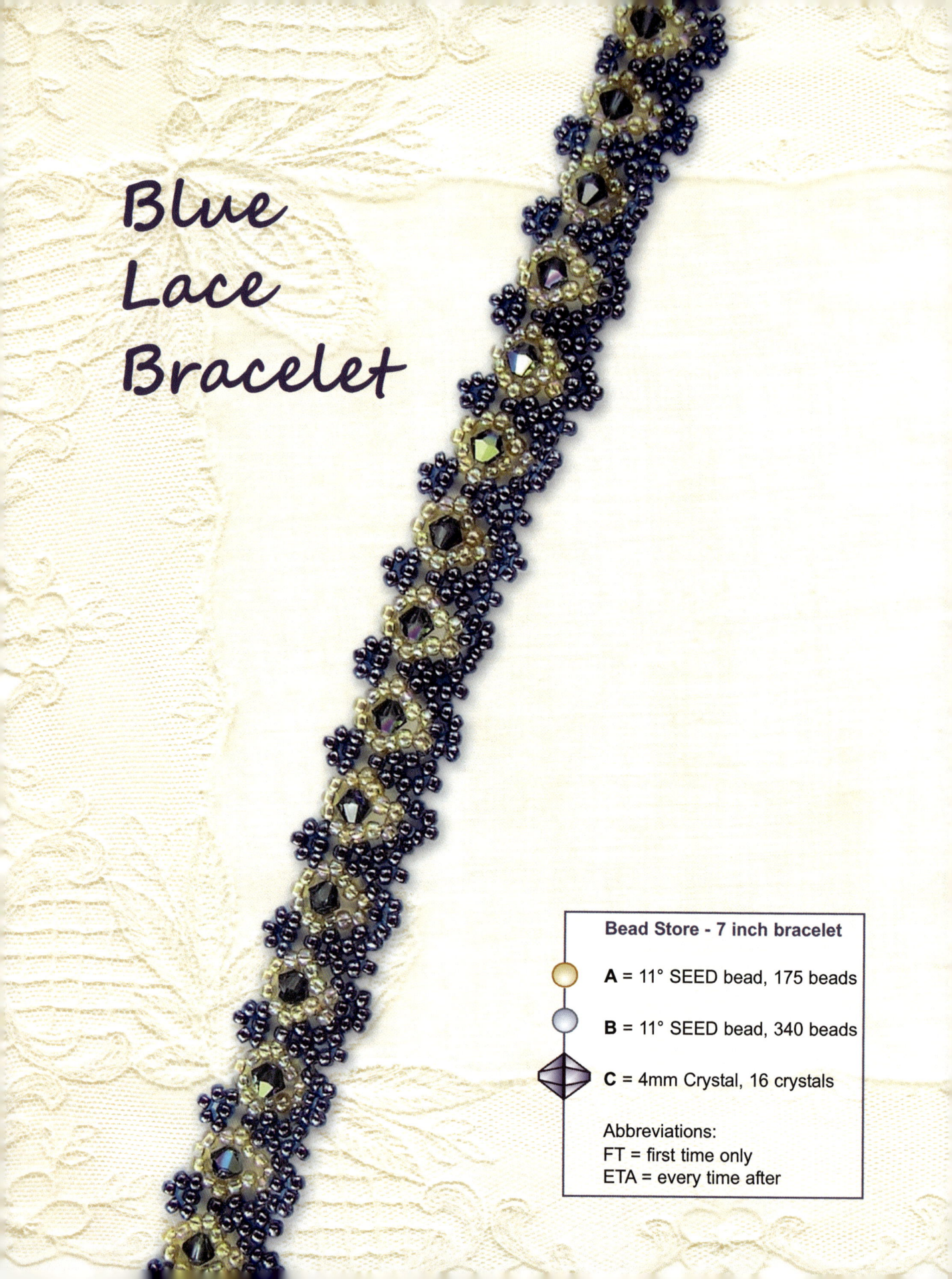

Bead Store - 7 inch bracelet

A = 11° SEED bead, 175 beads

B = 11° SEED bead, 340 beads

C = 4mm Crystal, 16 crystals

Abbreviations:
FT = first time only
ETA = every time after

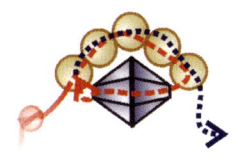

1. Pick up 5A, 1C, go with thread forward through the 5 A beads just added in this step.

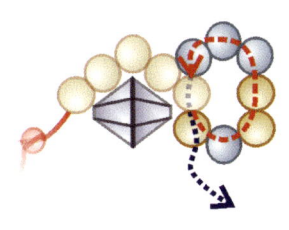

2. Pick up 1A, 1B, 2A, 3B, go with thread down through the 5th A bead added in step #1 and the 1st A bead just added in this step.

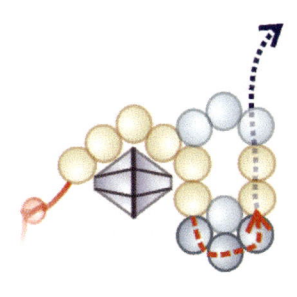

3. Pick up 3B, go with thread up through 2 A and the 1st B beads (of the 3B) added in step #2.

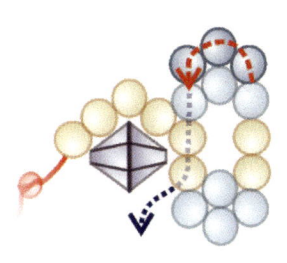

4. Pick up 3B, go with thread down through the 3rd B bead, step #2, the 5th A bead, step #1 and the 1st A bead, step #2.

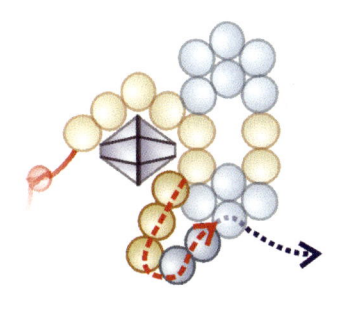

5. Pick up 3A, 2B, go with thread left to right through the 2nd B bead, step #3.

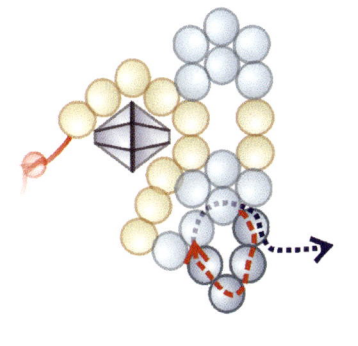

6. Pick up 4B, go with thread up through the 2nd B bead, step #5, left to right through the 2nd B bead, step #3 and down through the 1st B bead just added in this step.

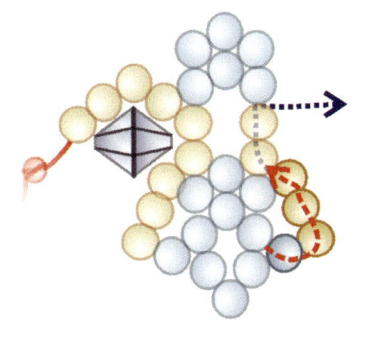

7. Pick up 1B, 3A, go with thread up through the 2 A beads (of the 2A) added in step #2.

blue lace bracelet pattern 39

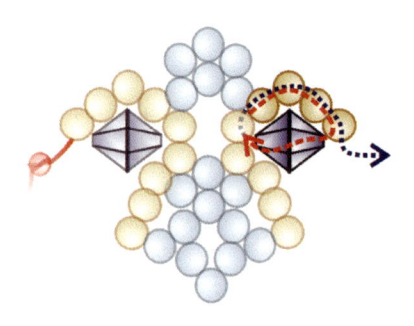

8. Pick up 4A, 1C, go with thread up through the 2nd A bead (of the 2A), step #2 and forward through the 4 A beads just added in this step.

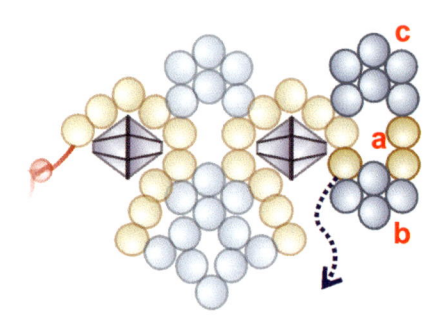

9. a) Pick up 1A, 1B, 2A, 3B, go with thread down through the 4th A bead added in step #8 (FT) or step #15 (ETA), and the 1st A bead just added in this step.
b) Pick up 3B, go with thread up through 2 A and the 1st B beads (of the 3B) added in in this step at (a).
c) Pick up 3B, go with thread down through the 3rd B bead (of the 3B), this step at (a), the 4th A bead, step #8 (FT) or step #15 (ETA) and the 1st A bead, this step at (a).

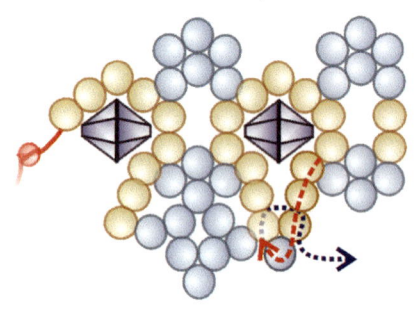

10. Pick up 3A, 1B, go with thread up through the 1st A bead, step #7 (FT) or step #14 (ETA) and down through the 3rd A bead just added in this step.

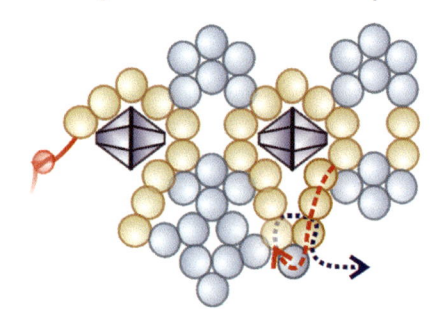

11. Pick up 6B, go with thread up through the B and 1st A beads added in step #7 (FT) or step #14 (ETA) and down through the 3rd A bead, step #10 and the 1st B bead just added in this step.

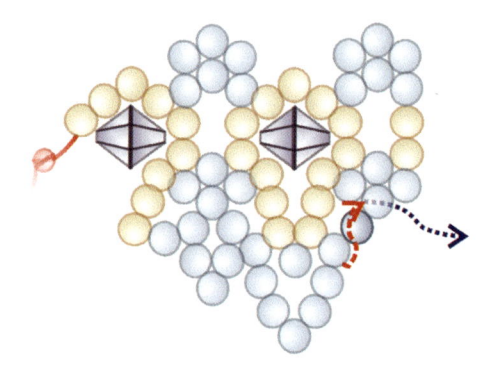

12. Pick up 1B, go with thread left to right through the 2nd B bead, step #9b.

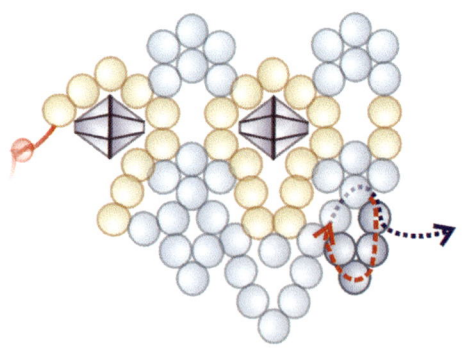

13. Pick up 4B, go with thread up through the 1 B bead, step #12, left to right through the 2nd B bead, step #9b and down through the 1st B bead just added in this step.

40 beaded bracelets pattern collection

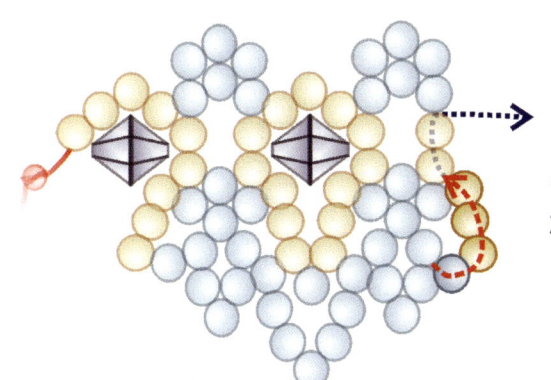

14. Pick up 1B, 3A, go with thread up through the 2 A beads, step #9a.

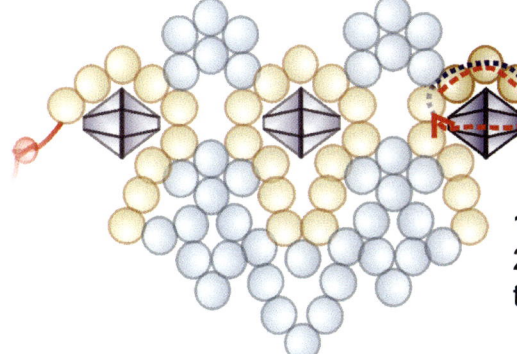

15. Pick up 4A, 1C, go with thread up through the 2nd A bead (of the 2A), step #9a and forward through the 4 A beads just added in this step.

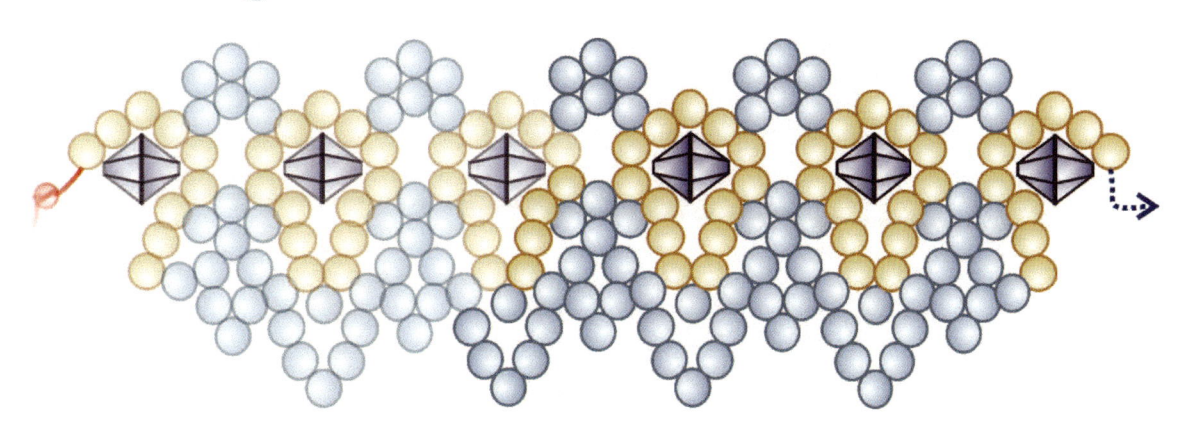

16. Continue bracelet by repeating steps #9 through #15 until the bracelet fits.

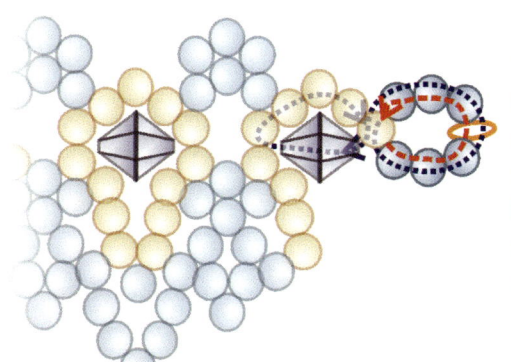

17. To add clasp, pick up 3A, clasp, 3A, go with thread down through 1 bead in bracelet. Continue with working thread around through the clasp beads several times. Weave the working thread into the bracelet and end. Repeat the clasp directions in the same manner on the other end after removing the stopper bead.

blue lace bracelet pattern

Crystal Edge Bracelet

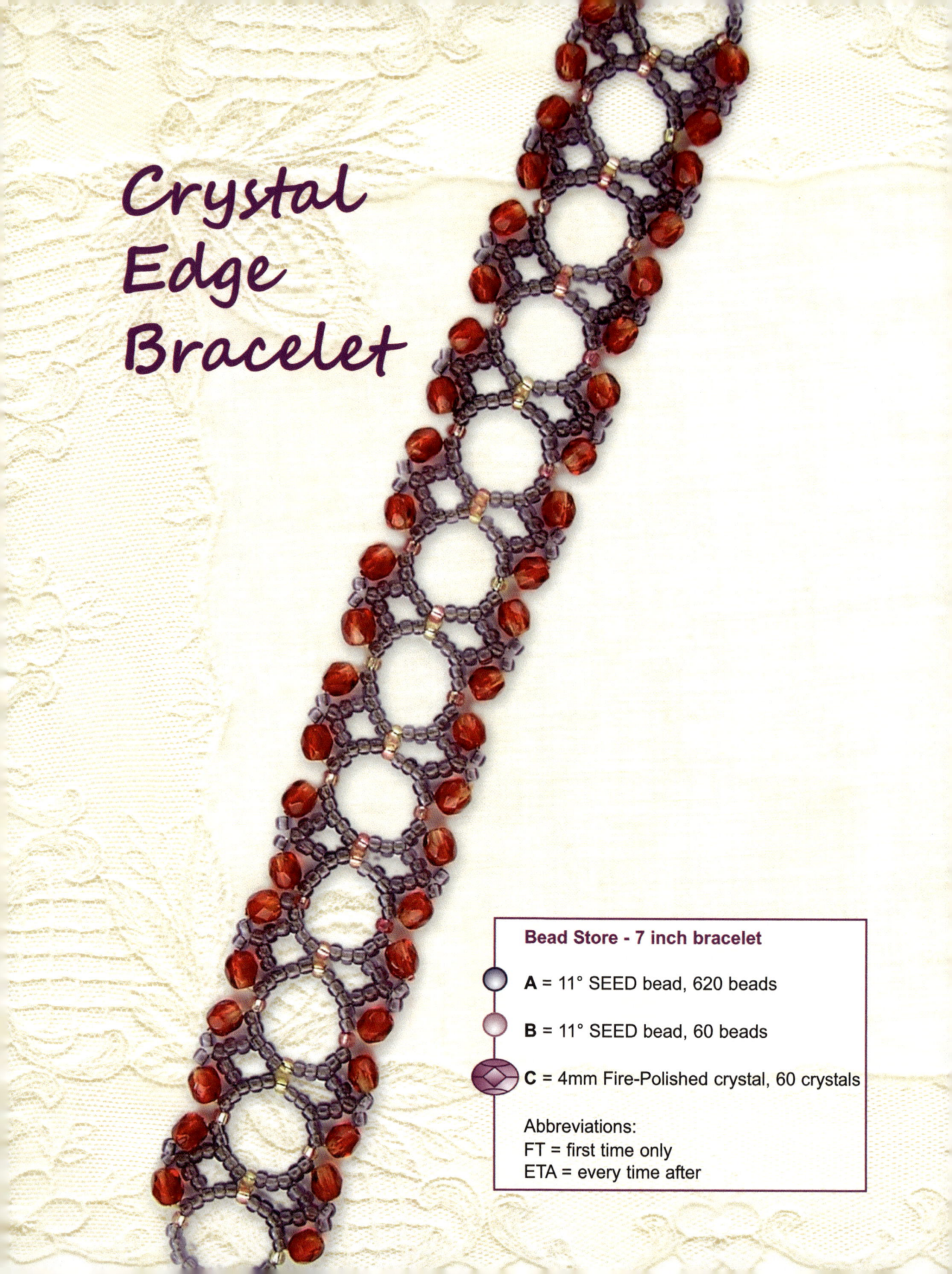

Bead Store - 7 inch bracelet

A = 11° SEED bead, 620 beads

B = 11° SEED bead, 60 beads

C = 4mm Fire-Polished crystal, 60 crystals

Abbreviations:
FT = first time only
ETA = every time after

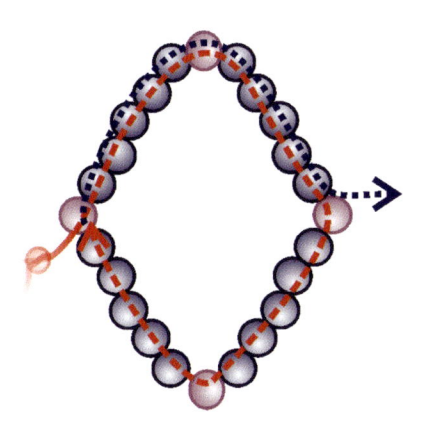

1. Pick up 1B, 5A, 1B, 5A, 1B, 5A, 1B, 5A, go with thread forward through the 1B, 5 A, 1B, 5 A beads just added.

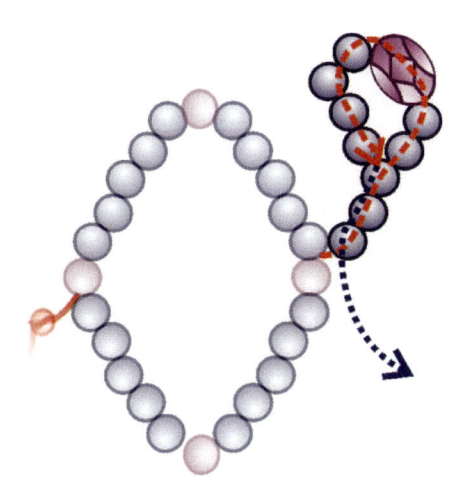

2. Pick up 5A, 1C, 4A, go with thread down through the 3rd, 2nd, 1st A beads (of the 5A) just added in this step.

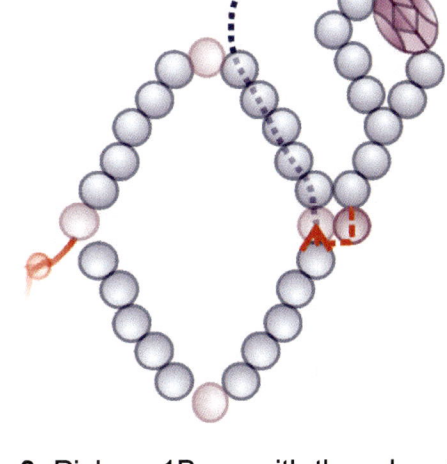

3. Pick up 1B, go with thread up through the 1 B and 5 A (of the 2nd set of 5A) added in step #1, FT or the 1st set of 5 A beads added in step #9, ETA.

4. Pick up 1C, 1A, go with thread down through the 2nd A bead (of the 4A) added in step #2.

crystal edge bracelet pattern 43

5. Pick up 2A, go with thread down through the 3rd, 4th, 5th A beads (of the 2nd set of 5A) added in step #1, (FT) or the 1st set of 5A added in step #9, (ETA), 1 B bead and 5 A beads (of the 3rd set of 5A) added in step #1, (FT) or of the 2nd set of 5A added in step #9, (ETA).

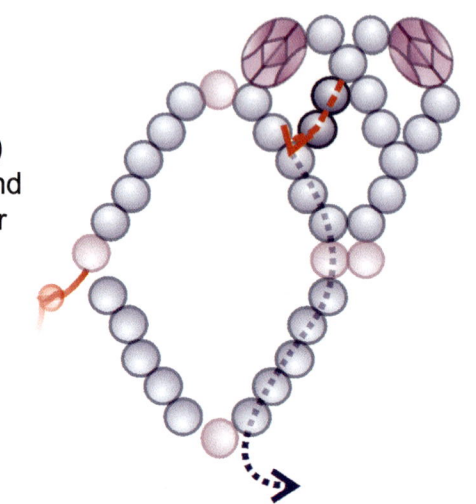

6. Pick up 1C, 4A, go with thread up through the 3rd, 2nd, 1st A beads (of the 3rd set of 5A) added in step #1, FT or the 2nd set of 5A, added in step #9, ETA, up through the B bead and down through the B bead added in step #3.

7. Pick up 5A, 1C, 1A, go with thread up through the 2nd A bead added in step #6.

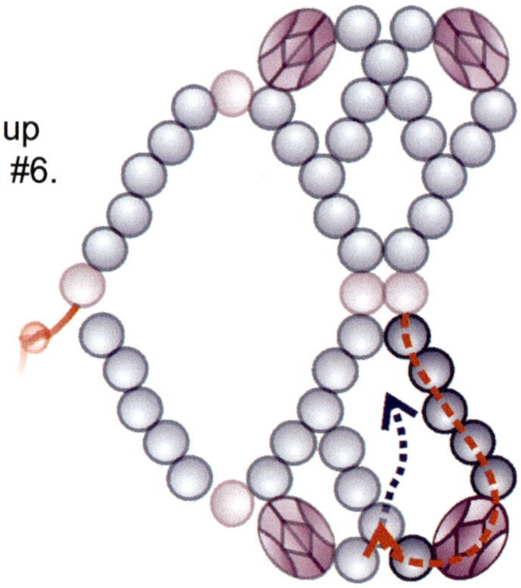

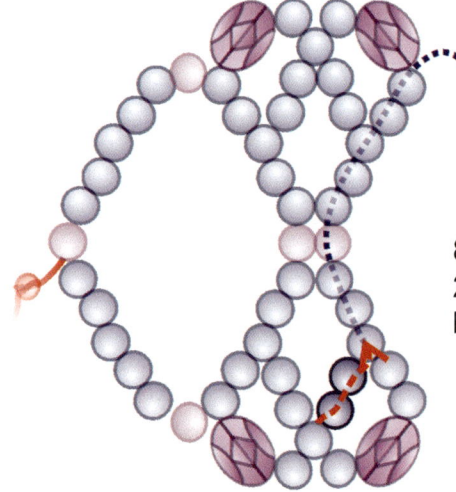

8. Pick up 2A, go with thread up through the 3rd, 2nd and 1st A beads added in step #7, the 1 B bead, step #3, and the 5 A beads added in step #2.

44 beaded bracelets pattern collection

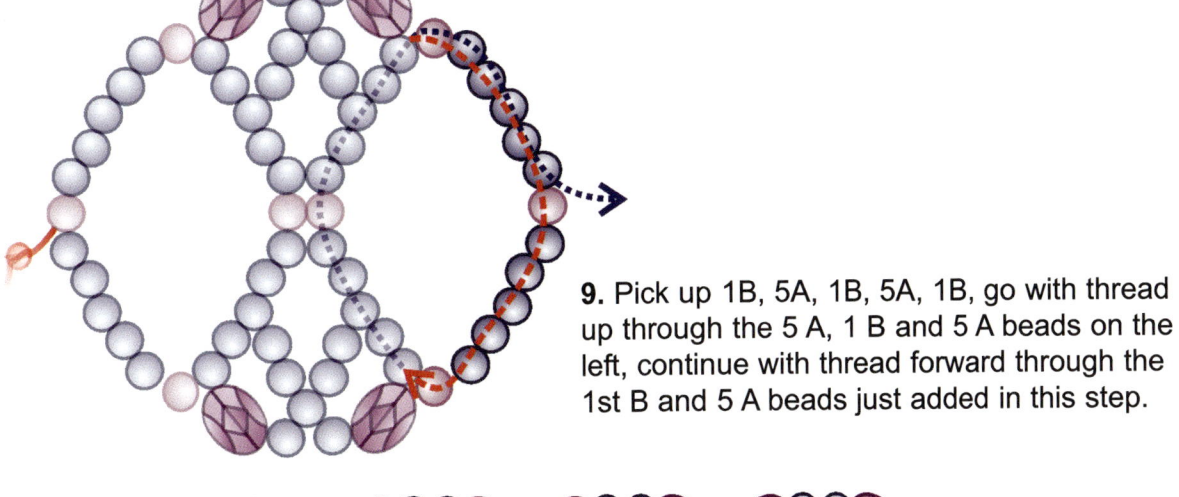

9. Pick up 1B, 5A, 1B, 5A, 1B, go with thread up through the 5 A, 1 B and 5 A beads on the left, continue with thread forward through the 1st B and 5 A beads just added in this step.

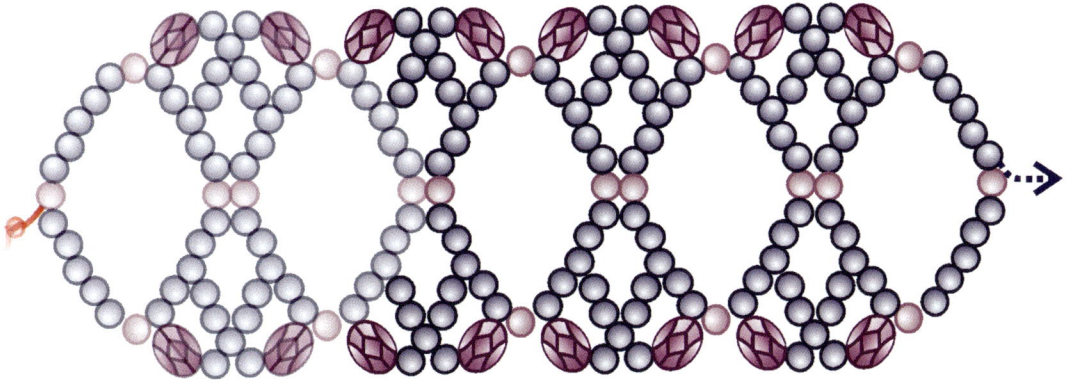

10. Continue bracelet by repeating steps #2 through #9 until the bracelet fits.

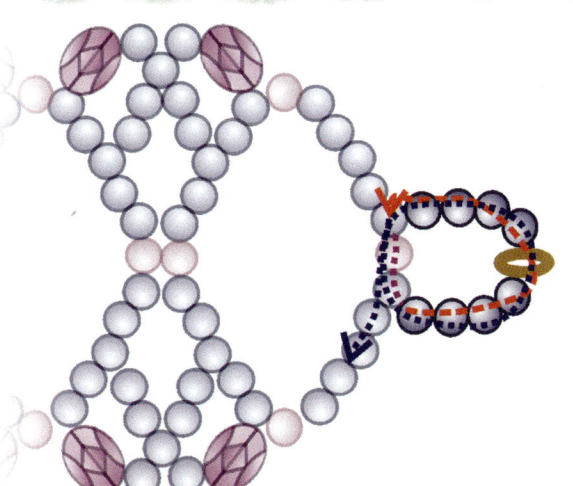

11. To add clasp, pick up 4A, clasp, 4A, go with thread down through 3 beads in bracelet. Continue with working thread around through the clasp beads several times. Weave the working thread into the bracelet and end. Repeat the clasp directions in the same manner on the other end after removing the stopper bead.

crystal edge bracelet pattern 45

Magenta Bronze Bracelet

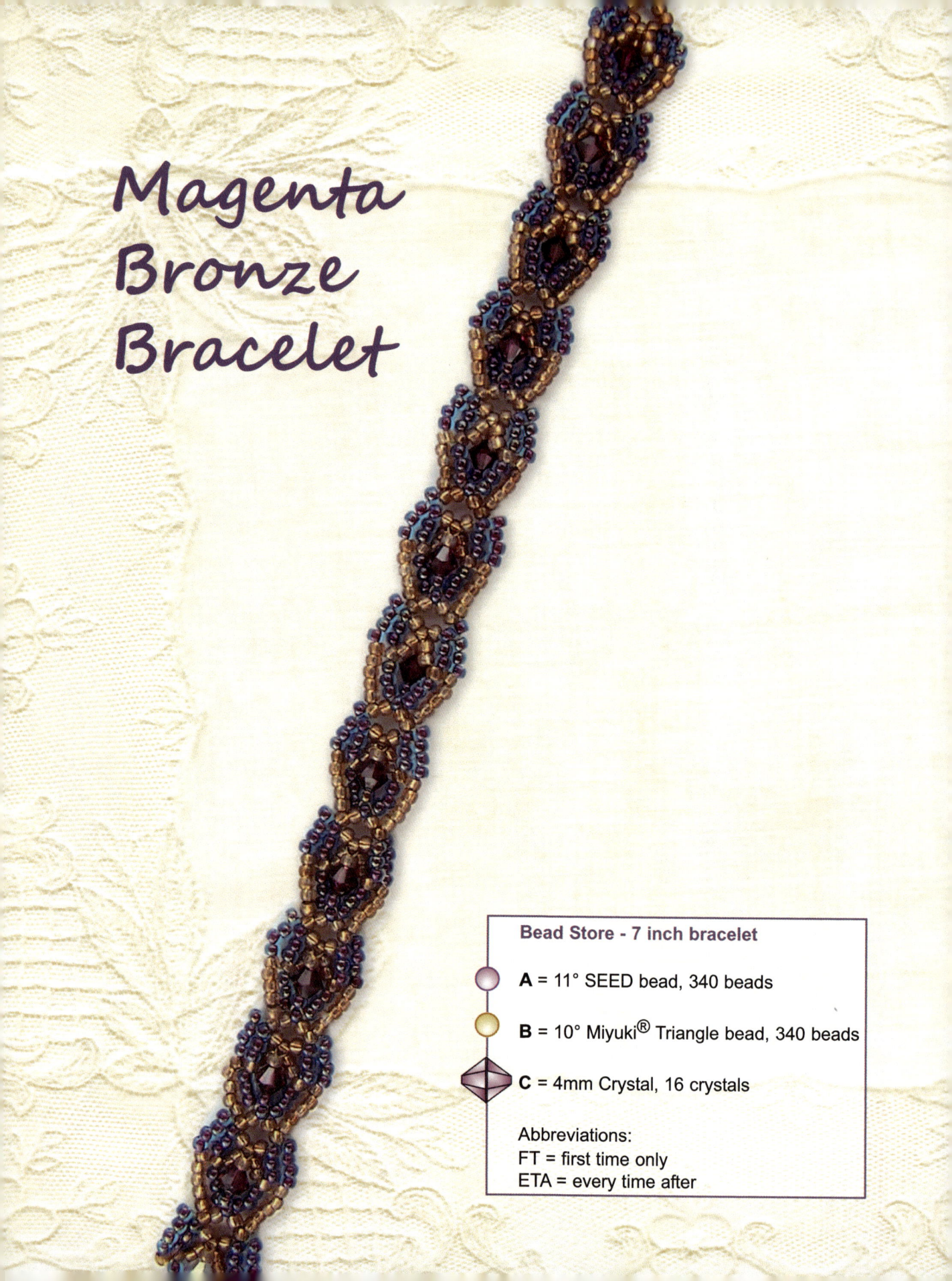

Bead Store - 7 inch bracelet

● **A** = 11° SEED bead, 340 beads

● **B** = 10° Miyuki® Triangle bead, 340 beads

◆ **C** = 4mm Crystal, 16 crystals

Abbreviations:
FT = first time only
ETA = every time after

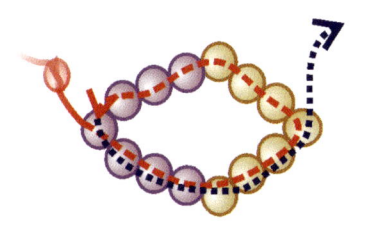

1. Row 1, Pick up 4B, 7A, 3B, go with thread forward through the 4 B beads and the 1st through 4th A beads just added.

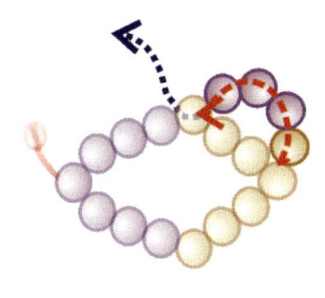

2. Pick up 1A, 3B, go with thread right to left through the 7th A bead added in step #1 or #8.

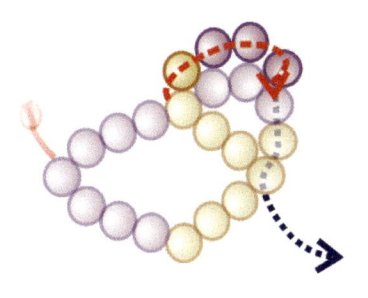

3. Pick up 1A, 3B, go with thread down through the 1st B bead and A bead, step #2 and the 4th A bead added in step #1 or #8.

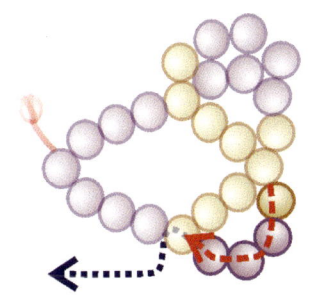

4. Pick up 1A, 3B, go with thread right to left through the 1st A bead added in step #1 or #8.

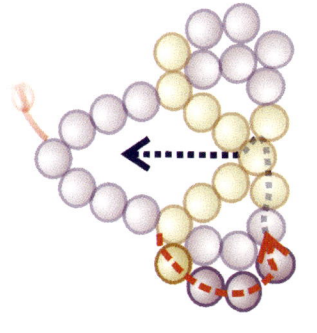

5. Pick up 1A, 3B, go with thread up through the 1st B bead and A bead added in step #4 and the 4th A bead, step #1 or #8.

magenta bronze bracelet pattern 47

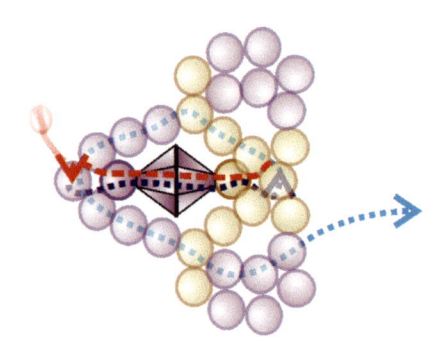

6. Pick up 1A, 1C, 1B, go with thread down through the 1st B bead (step #1, FT) or the B bead (step #7, ETA), left to right through the B, C and A beads added in this step. Continue with working thread around through beads as shown in illustration, coming out with thread at the 1st B bead added in step #4.

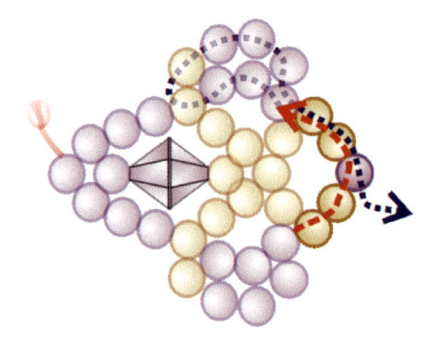

7. Pick up 2A, 1B, 2A, go with thread right to left through the 3 B beads, step #2, the 7th A bead, step #1 or #8, the 1 A and 3 B beads, step #3, the 1st B bead, step #2 and the 2nd set of 2 A and 1 B beads just added in this step.

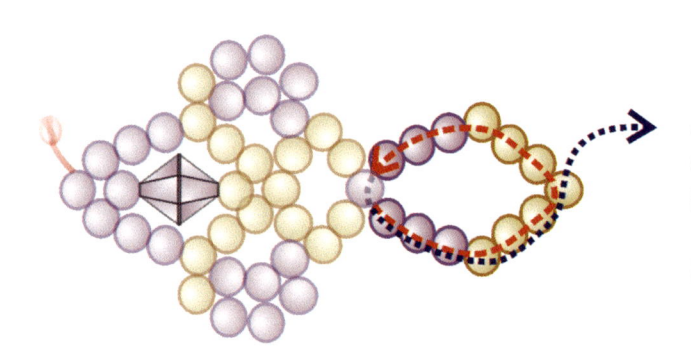

8. Pick up 3B, 7A, 3B, go with thread down through the B bead added in step #7 and forward through the 1st set of 3 B beads and the 1st through 4th A beads just added in this step.

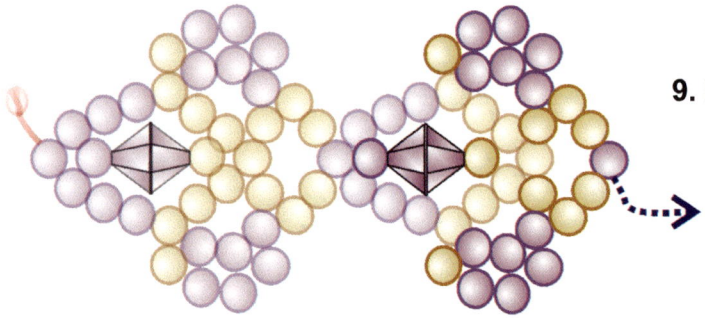

9. Repeat steps #2 through #7.

48 beaded bracelets pattern collection

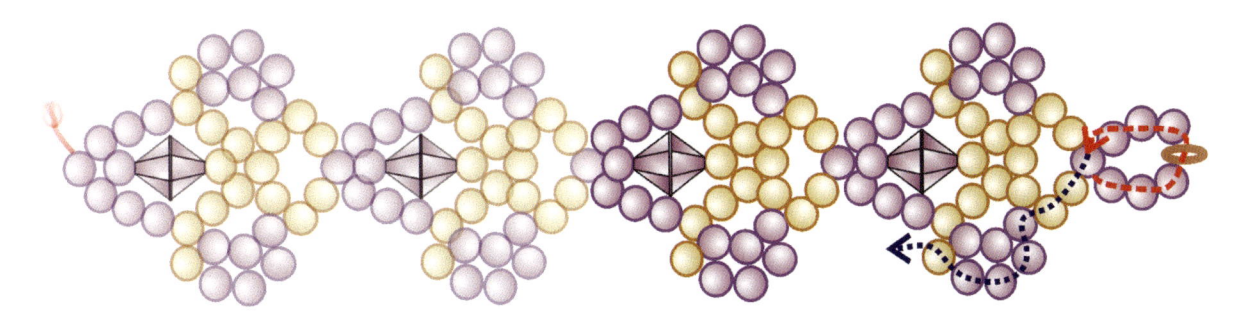

10. To add clasp, pick up 3B, clasp, 3B, go with thread down through 1 B bead in bracelet. Continue with working thread around through the clasp beads several times. Continue with working thread through bracelet as shown, coming out with thread at the 1st A bead added in the last repeat of step #5.

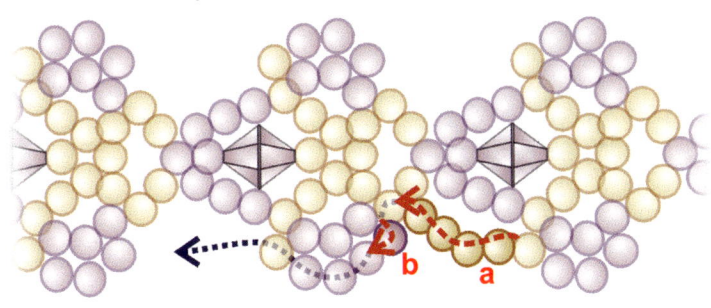

11. Row 2
a) Pick up 4A, go with thread right to left through the 1st A bead added in a repeat of step #7.
b) Pick up 1B, go with thread right to left through the 3 B and 1 A beads added in a repeat of step #5.

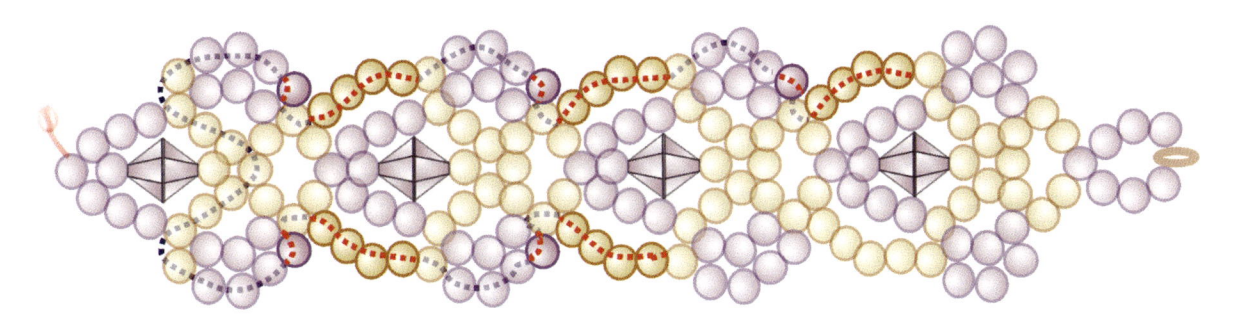

12. Continue to repeat steps #11 (a and b) right to left across to the other end of bracelet. Weave through bracelet to the other side and repeat step #11 (b and a) in the same manner left to right across to the other end. Please note: When you are doing step #11(b) in this direction, you are only going through the 2nd A bead of the 2nd set of A beads, step #7. Repeat the clasp directions in the same manner as step #10 on the other end after removing the stopper bead.

magenta bronze bracelet pattern

Lilac Blue Bracelet

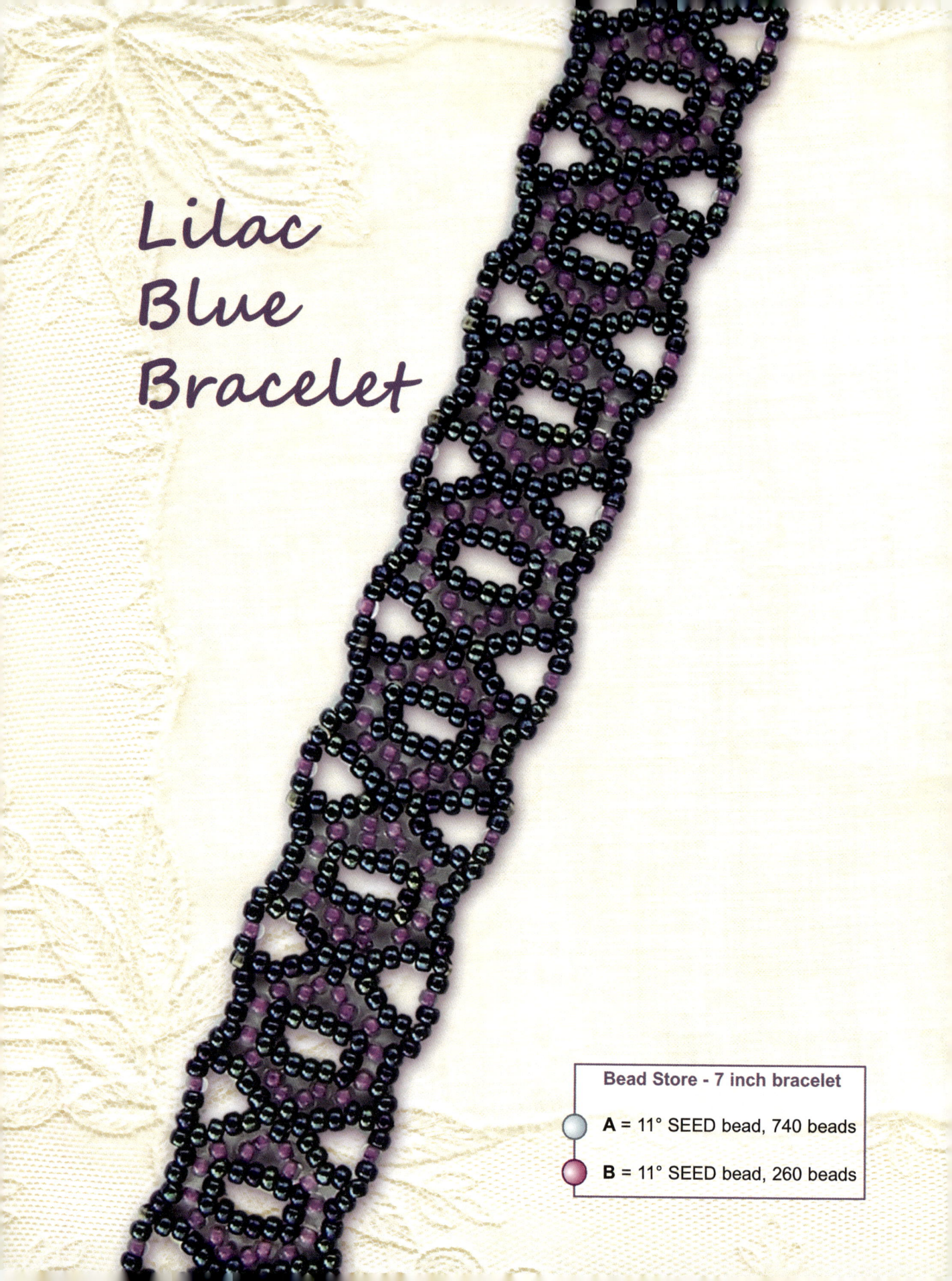

Bead Store - 7 inch bracelet

A = 11° SEED bead, 740 beads

B = 11° SEED bead, 260 beads

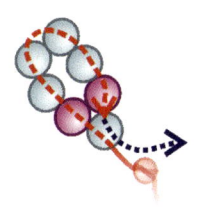

1. Pick up 1A, 1B, 4A, 1B, go with thread down through the 1st A bead just added.

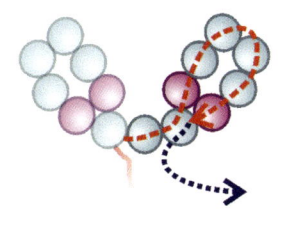

2. Pick up 2A, 1B, 4A, 1B, go with thread down through the 2nd A bead (of the 2A) just added in this step.

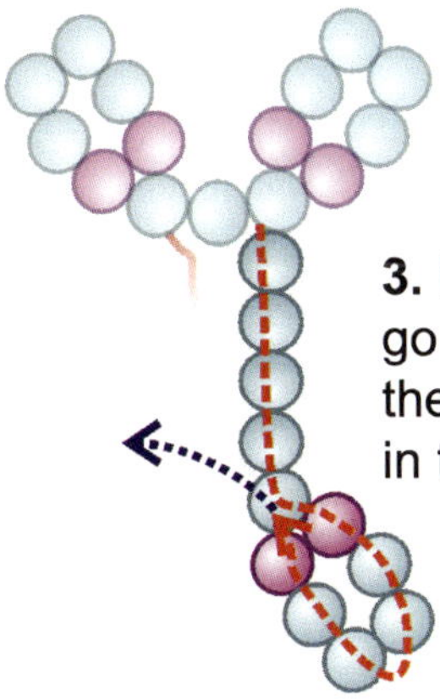

3. Pick up 5A, 1B, 4A, 1B, go with thread up through the 5th A bead just added in this step.

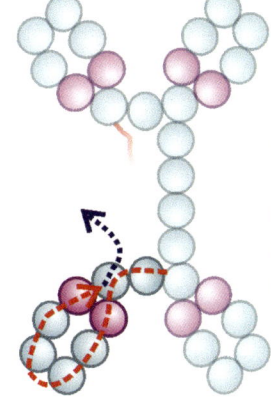

4. Pick up 2A, 1B, 4A, 1B, go with thread up through the 2nd A (of the 2A) just added in this step.

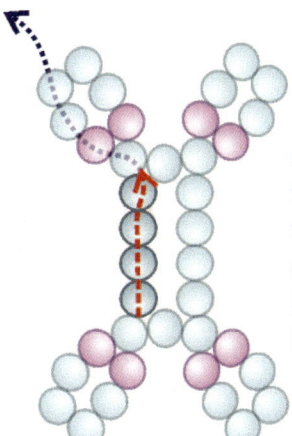

5. Pick up 4A, go with thread forward (up) through the 1st A, 1st B and the 1st and 2nd A beads (of the 4A) added in step #1.

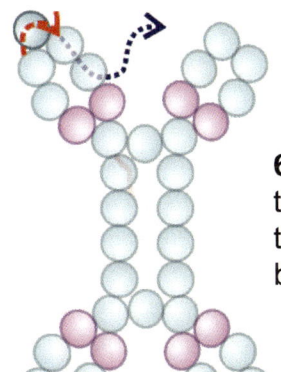

6. Pick up 1A, go with thread forward (down) through the 3rd and 4th A beads added in step #1.

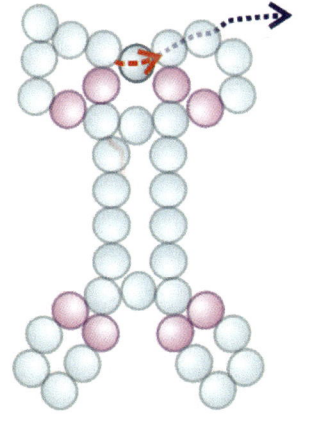

7. Pick up 1A, go with thread forward (up) through the 1st and 2nd A beads (of the 4A) added in step #2.

lilac blue bracelet pattern 51

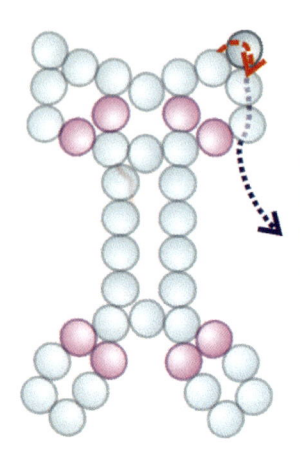

8. Pick up 1A, go with thread forward (down) through the 3rd and 4th A beads (of the 4A) added in step #2.

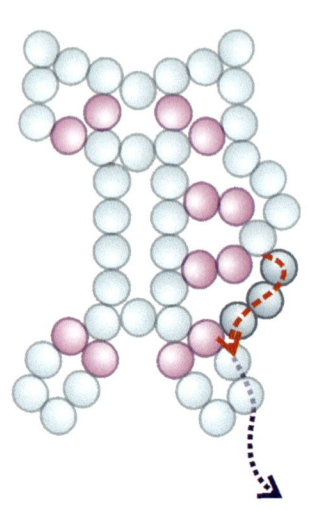

9. Pick up 4A, 2B, go with thread up through the 3rd and 2nd A beads (of the 5A) added in step #3.

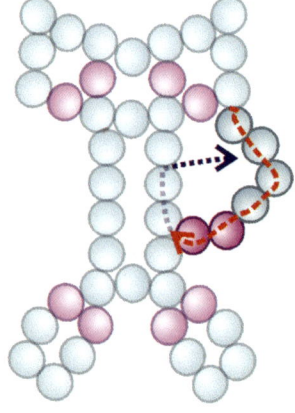

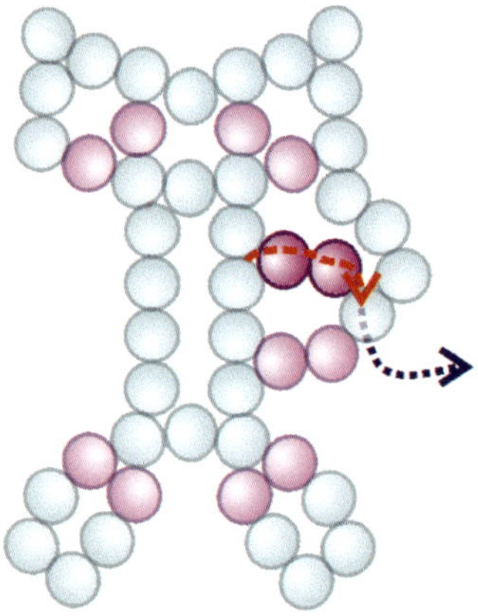

10. Pick up 2B, go with thread forward (down) through the 4th A bead added in step #9.

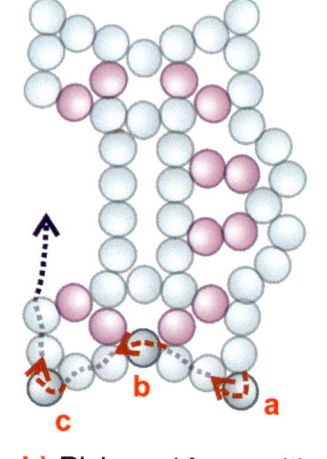

11. Pick up 3A, go with thread forward (down) through the 1st and 2nd A beads (of the 4A) added in step #3.

12. a) Pick up 1A, go with thread forward (up) through the 3rd and 4th A beads (of the 4A) added in step #3.
b) Pick up 1A, go with thread forward (down) through the 1st and 2nd A beads (of the 4A) added in step #4.
c) Pick up 1A, go with thread forward (up) through the 3rd and 4th A beads (of the 4A) added in step #4.

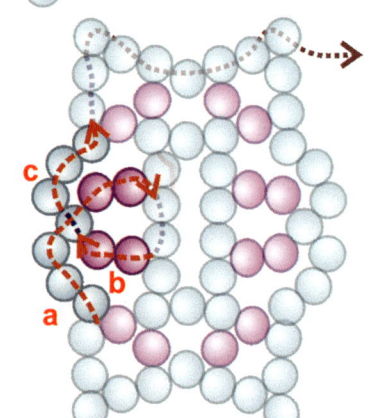

13. a) Pick up 4A, 2B, go with thread down through the 3rd and 2nd A beads added in step #5.
b) Pick up 2B, go with thread forward (up) through the 4th A bead added in this step at (a).
c) Pick up 3A, go with thread up through the 1st and 2nd A beads, (of the 4A), step #1, the A bead (step #6), the 3rd and 4th A beads (of the 4A), step #1, 1 A bead (step #7), the 1st and 2nd A beads (of the 4A), step #2, and the 1A bead, step #8.

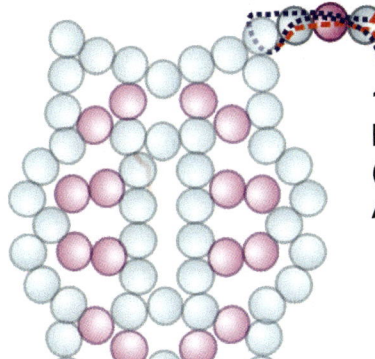

14. Pick up 1A, 1B, 2A, go with thread down through the 1st A bead (of the 2A), 1 B and 1st A, just added in this step, forward (down) through the A bead (step #8) and forward through the 1 A, 1 B and 2 A beads just added in this step.

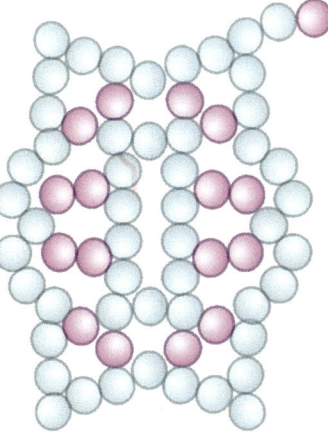

15. Pick up 2A, 1B, 3A, 1B, 4A, 1B, go with thread down through the 3rd A bead (of the 3A) just added in this step.

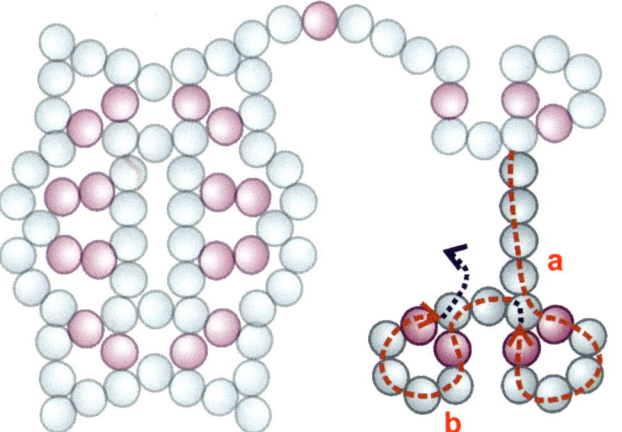

16. a) Pick up 5A, 1B, 4A, 1B, go with thread up through the 5th A bead just added in this step.
b) Pick up 2A, 1B, 4A, 1B, go with thread up through the 2nd A (of the 2A) just added in this step.

17. Pick up 4A, go with thread up through the 1st A bead (of the 3A) added in step #15.

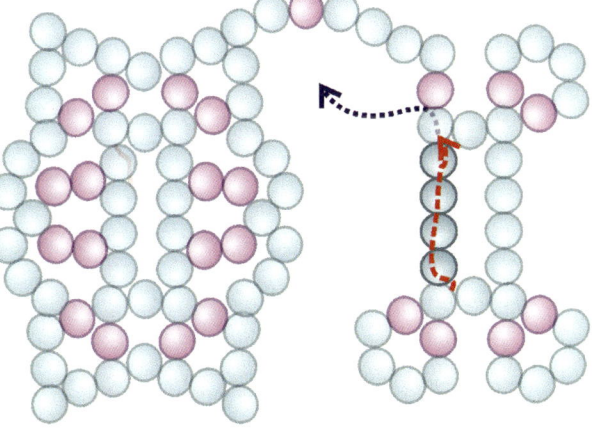

lilac blue bracelet pattern

18. Pick up 1B, 2A, go with thread forward (left to right) through the 1st and 2nd A beads, step #15.

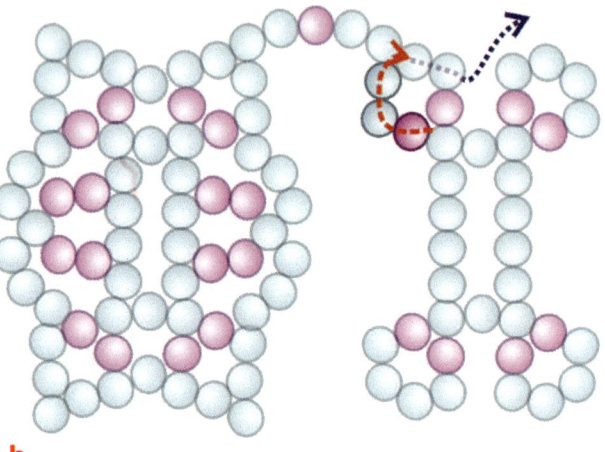

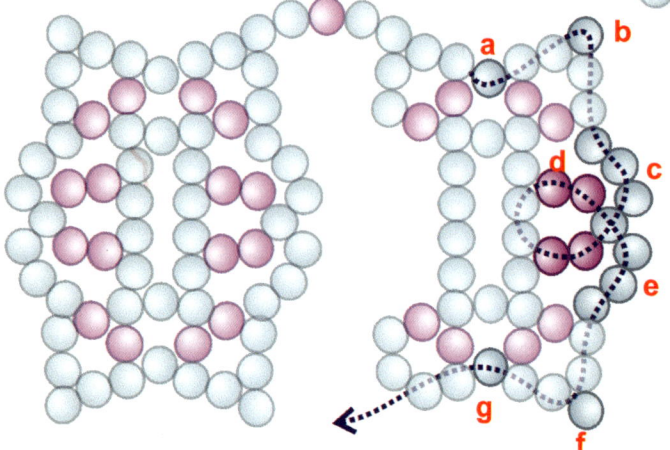

19. a) Pick up 1A, go with thread forward (up) through the 1st and 2nd A beads (of the 4A) added in step #16a.
b) Pick up 1A, go with thread forward (down) through the 3rd and 4th A beads (of the 4A) added in step #15.
c) Pick up 4A, 2B, go with thread up through the 3rd and 2nd A beads (of the 5A) added in step #16a.
d) Pick up 2B, go with thread forward (down) through the 4th A bead added in this step at (c).
e) Pick up 3A, go with thread forward (down) through the 1st and 2nd A beads (of the 4A) added in step #3.
f) Pick up 1A, go with thread forward (up) through the 3rd and 4th A beads (of the 4A) added in step #16a.
g) Pick up 1A, go with thread forward (down) through the 1st and 2nd A beads (of the 4A) added in step #16b.

20. Pick up 2A, 1B, 1A, go with thread forward (down) through the A bead added in step #12a, left to right through the beads added in this step and forward (up) through the 3rd and 4th A beads (of the 4A) added in step #16b.

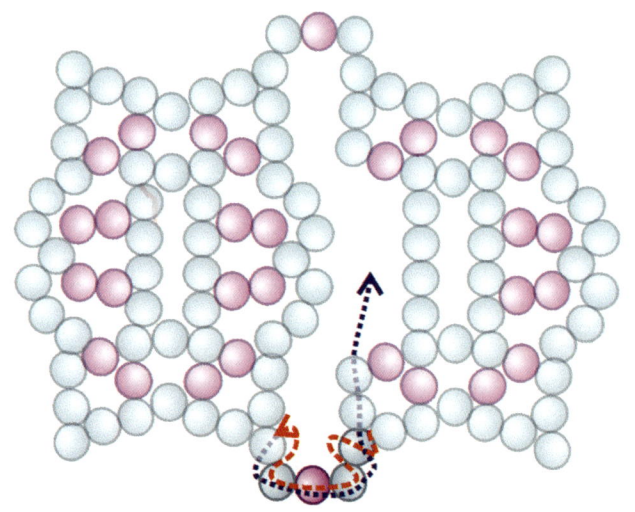

54 beaded bracelets pattern collection

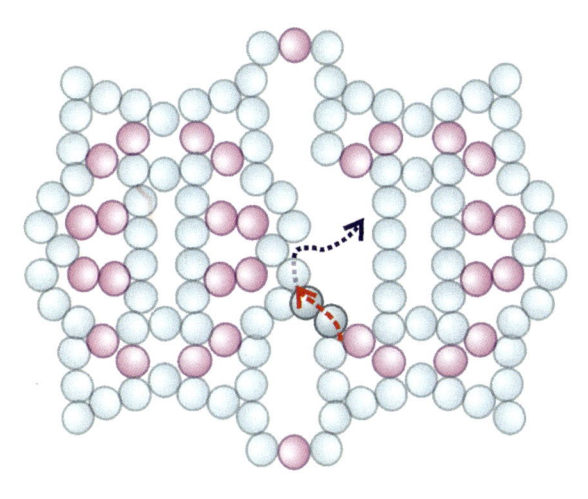

21. Pick up 2A, go with thread up through the 1st A bead added in step #11 or #19e.

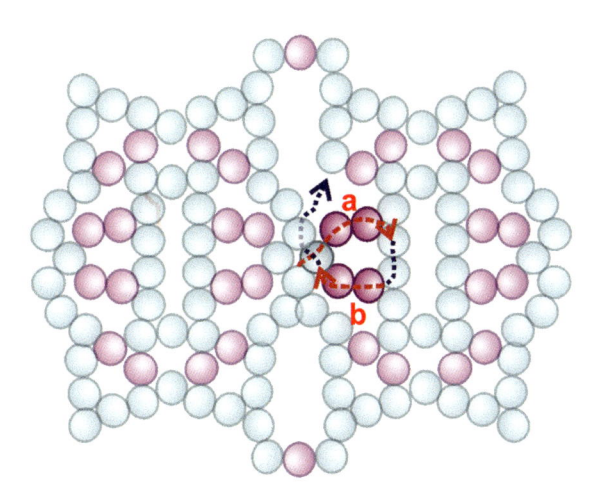

22. a) Pick up 1A, 2B, go with thread down through the 3rd and 2nd A beads, step #17.
b) Pick up 2B, go with thread up through the A bead added in this step at (a) and the 3rd A bead, step #9 or #19c.

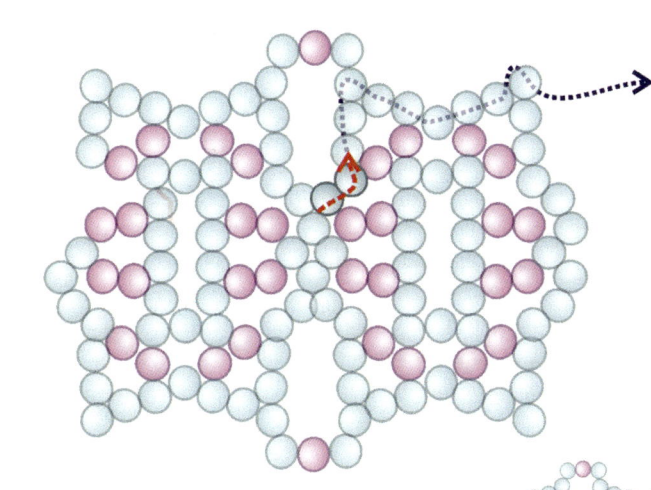

23. Pick up 2A, go with thread forward through the 2 A beads, step #18, the last A bead, step #14, the 1st and 2nd A beads, step #15, 1 A bead, step #19a, the 1st and 2nd A beads (of the 4A), step #15 and the 1 A bead, step #19b.

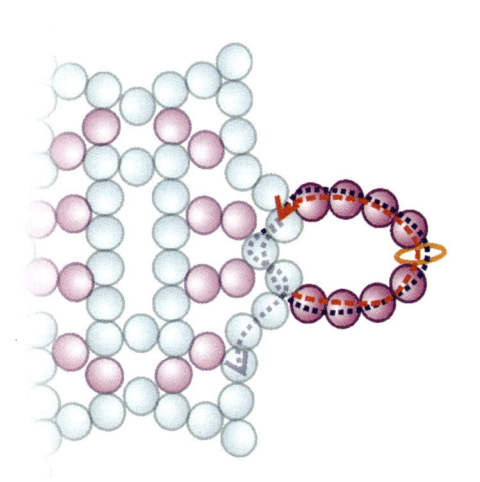

24. Continue bracelet by repeating steps #14 through #23, until the bracelet fits.

25. To add clasp, pick up 4B, clasp, 4B, go with thread down through 3 center beads in bracelet. Continue with working thread around through the clasp beads several times. Weave the working thread into the bracelet and end. Repeat the clasp directions in the same manner on the other end after removing the stopper bead.

lilac blue bracelet pattern 55

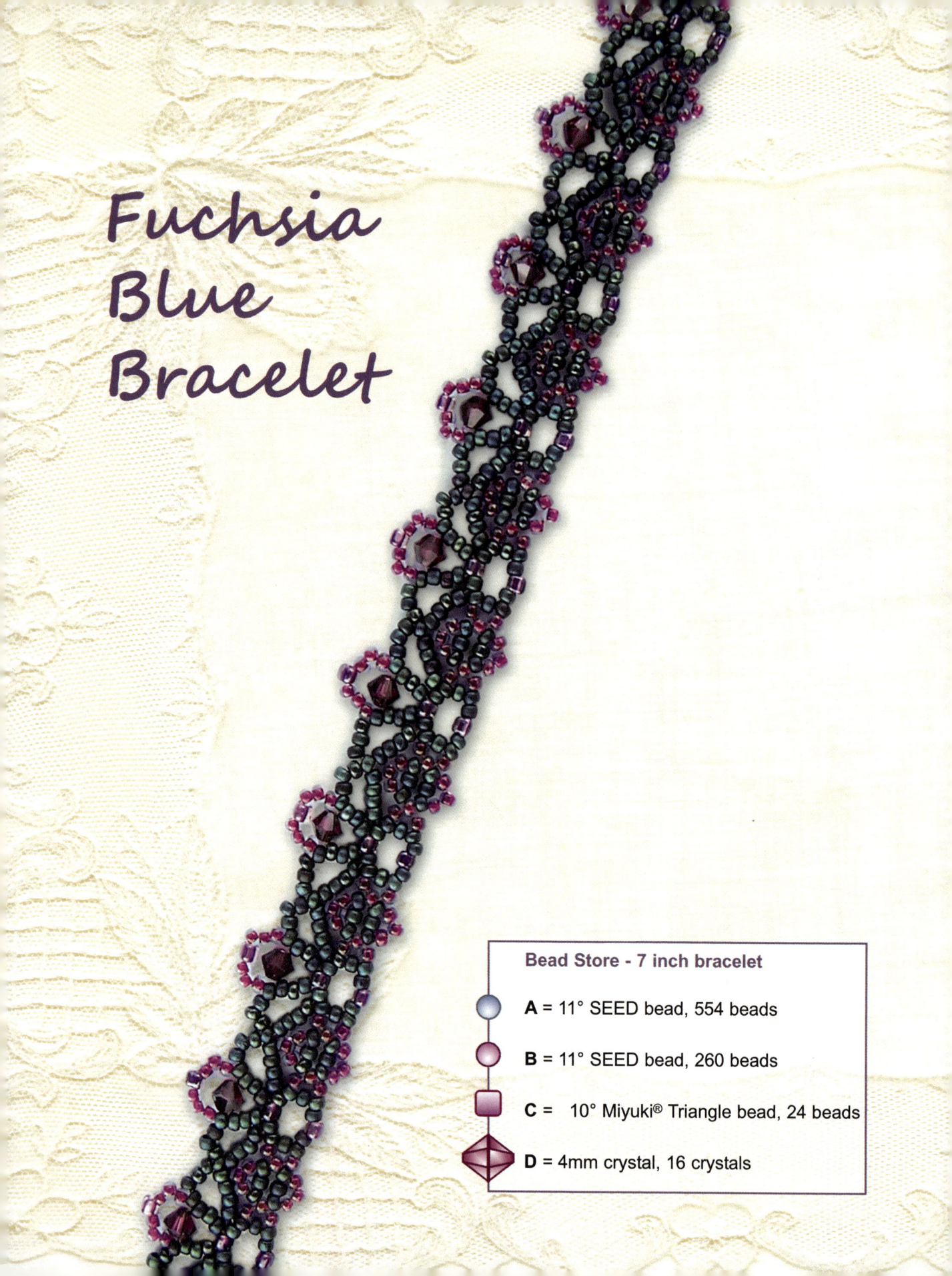

Fuchsia Blue Bracelet

Bead Store - 7 inch bracelet

A = 11° SEED bead, 554 beads

B = 11° SEED bead, 260 beads

C = 10° Miyuki® Triangle bead, 24 beads

D = 4mm crystal, 16 crystals

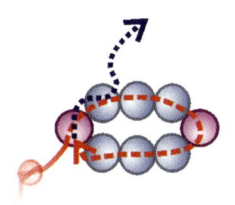

1. Pick up 1B, 3A, 1B, 3A, go with thread forward through the 1st B and 1st A beads just added in this step.

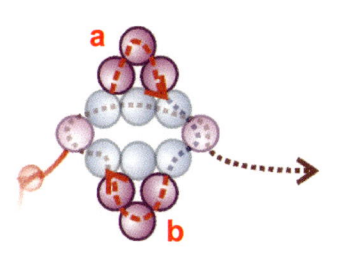

2. a) Pick up 3B, go with thread forward through the 3rd A bead (of the 1st 3A), the 2nd B bead and the 1st A bead (of the 2nd 3A) added in step #1.
b) Pick up 3B, go with thread forward through the 3rd A (of the 2nd 3A), 1 B, 3 A beads (of the 1st 3A) and 1 B bead added in step #1.

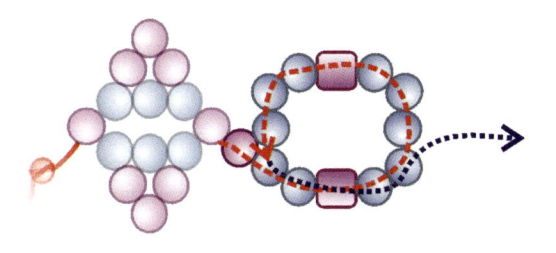

3. Pick up 1B, 2A, 1C, 5A, 1C, 3A, go with thread forward through 2 A, 1 C and the 1st, 2nd A beads (of the 5A) just added in this step.

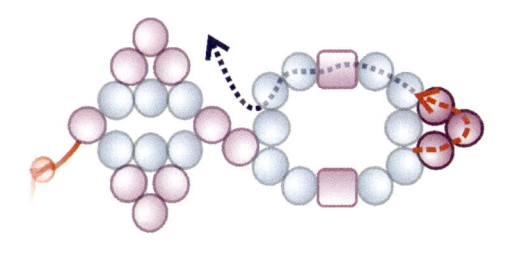

4. Pick up 3B, go with thread forward through the 4th and 5th A beads (of the 5A), 1 C and the 1st, 2nd A beads (of the 3A) added in step #3.

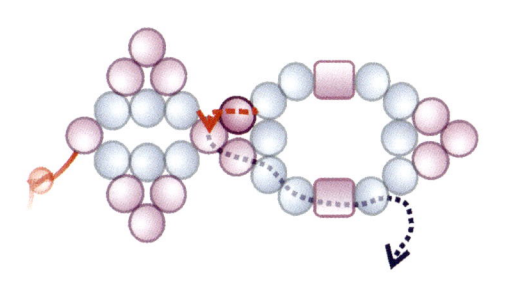

5. Pick up 1B, go with thread down through the B bead, step #1 or #10, forward through 1 B, 2 A, 1 C and the 1st A bead (of the 5A) added in step #3.

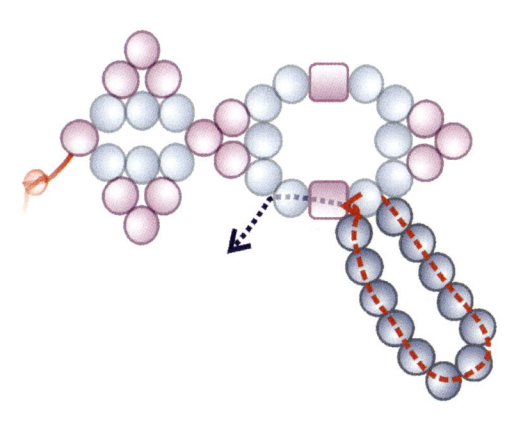

6. Pick up 12A, go with thread right to left through the 1st C bead and the 2nd A bead (of the 2A) added in step #3.

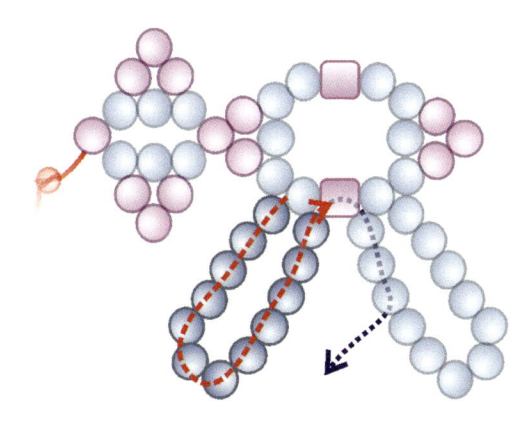

7. Pick up 12A, go with thread left to right through the 1st C bead, step #3 and the 12th, 11th and 10th A beads added in step #6.

fuchsia blue bracelet pattern 57

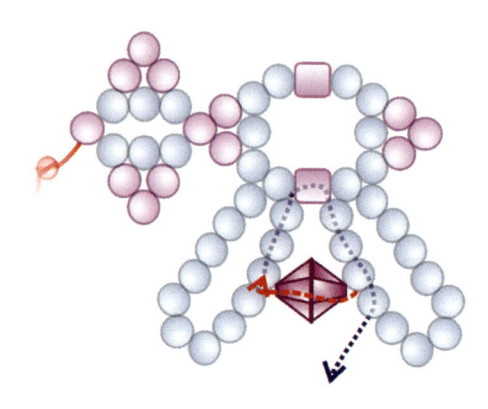

8. Pick up 1D, go with thread up through the 10th, 11th and 12th A beads, step #7 or the 5th, 6th and 7th A beads, step #14, left to right through the 1st C bead, step #3 or the step #12a, repeat of step #3 and down through the 12th, 11th, 10th and 9th A beads, step #6 or the step #12d, repeat of step #6.

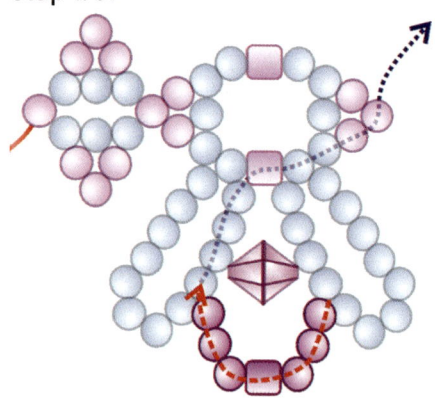

9. Pick up 3B, 1C, 3B, go with thread up through the 9th, 10th, 11th and 12th A beads, step #7 or the 4th, 5th, 6th, and 7th A beads, step #14, forward through the 1st C bead, the 1st and 2nd A beads (of the 5A), step #3 or the step #12a, repeat of step #3 and the 1st and 2nd B beads, step #4 or the step #12b, repeat of step #4.

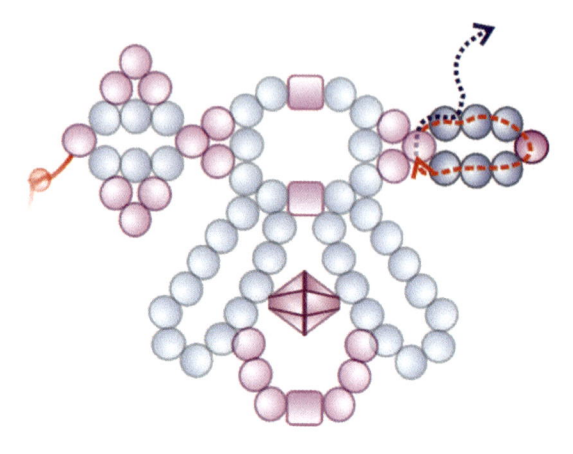

10. Pick up 3A, 1B, 3A, go with thread up through the 2nd B bead, step #4 and forward through the 1st A bead just added in this step.

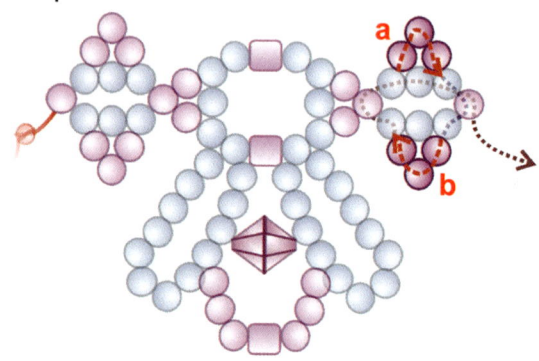

11. a) Pick up 3B, go with thread forward through the 3rd A bead (of the second 3A), 1 B bead and the 1st A bead (of the 2nd 3A) added in step #10.
b) Pick up 3B, go with thread forward through the 3rd A bead (of the second 3A), step #10, the B bead, step #4, the first 3 A beads and 1 B bead, step #10.

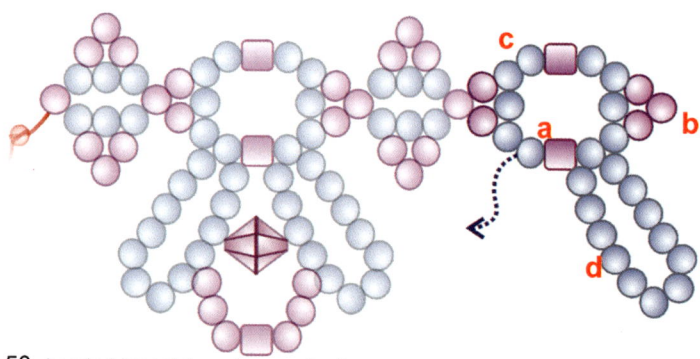

12. a) Repeat step #3
b) Repeat step #4
c) Repeat step #5
d) Repeat step #6

58 beaded bracelets pattern collection

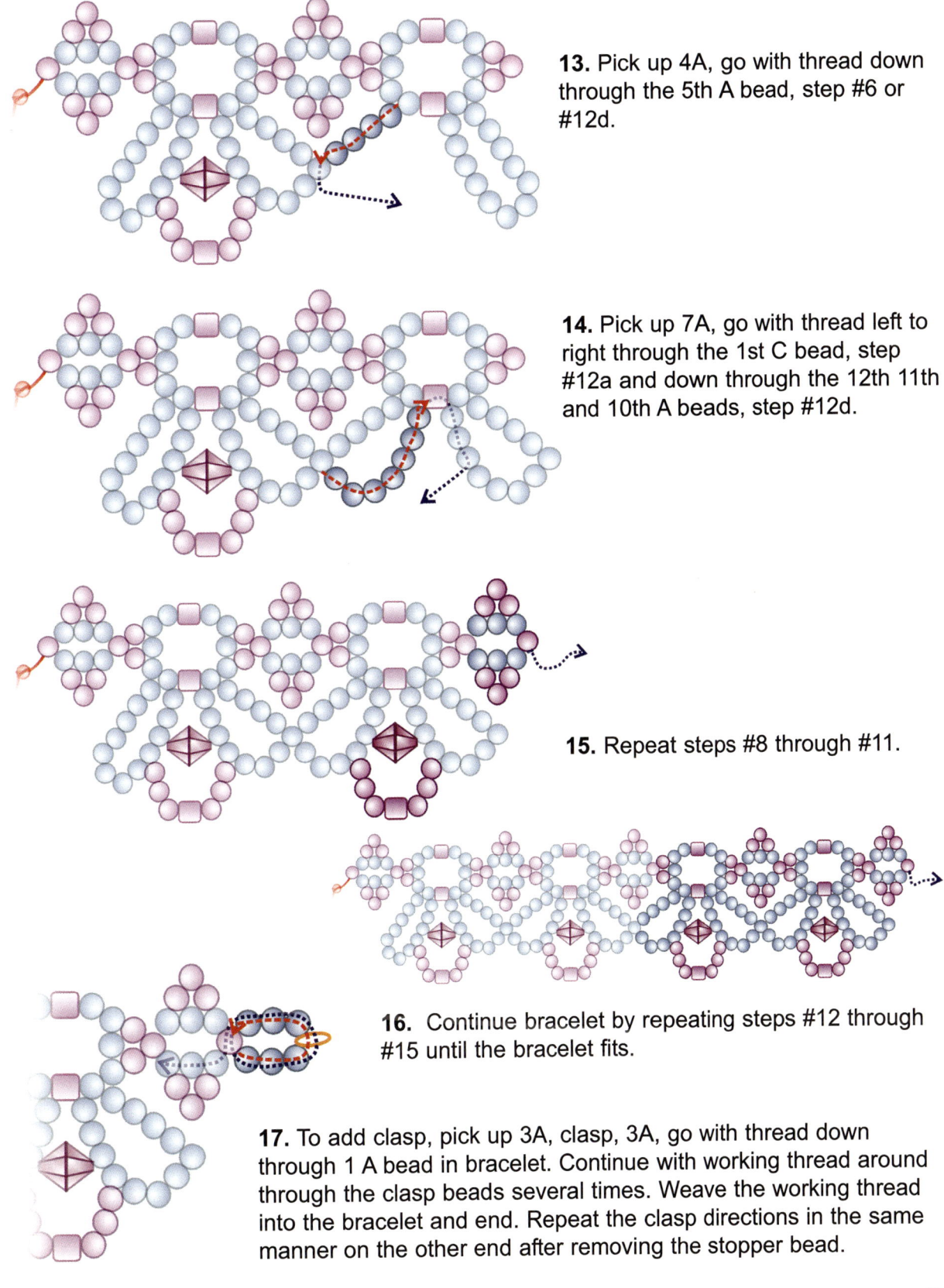

13. Pick up 4A, go with thread down through the 5th A bead, step #6 or #12d.

14. Pick up 7A, go with thread left to right through the 1st C bead, step #12a and down through the 12th 11th and 10th A beads, step #12d.

15. Repeat steps #8 through #11.

16. Continue bracelet by repeating steps #12 through #15 until the bracelet fits.

17. To add clasp, pick up 3A, clasp, 3A, go with thread down through 1 A bead in bracelet. Continue with working thread around through the clasp beads several times. Weave the working thread into the bracelet and end. Repeat the clasp directions in the same manner on the other end after removing the stopper bead.

fuchsia blue bracelet pattern 59

Gold Wine Bracelet

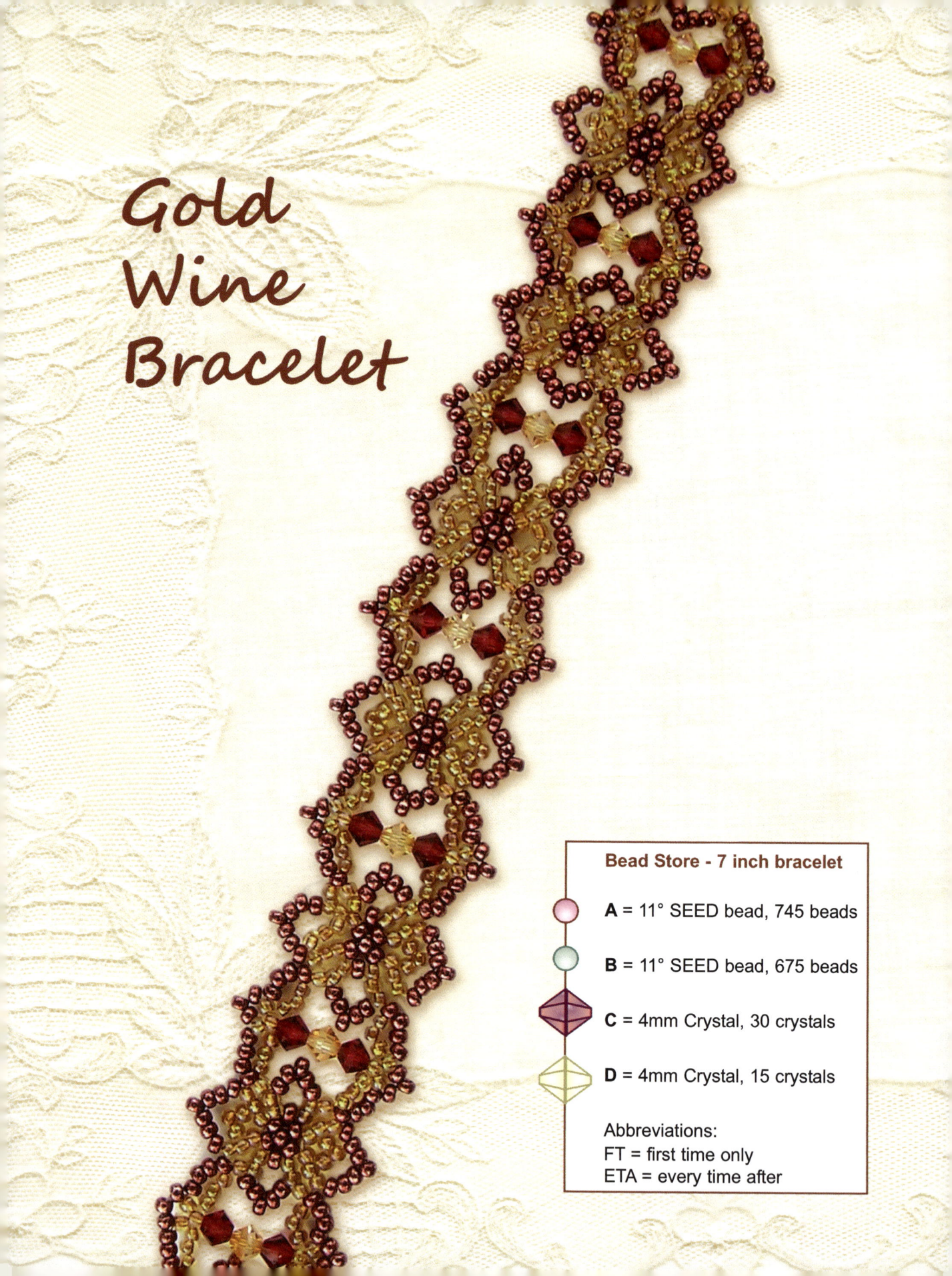

Bead Store - 7 inch bracelet

- **A** = 11° SEED bead, 745 beads
- **B** = 11° SEED bead, 675 beads
- **C** = 4mm Crystal, 30 crystals
- **D** = 4mm Crystal, 15 crystals

Abbreviations:
FT = first time only
ETA = every time after

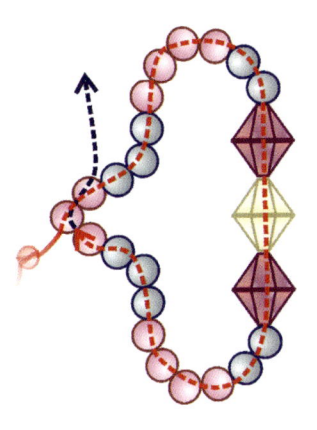

1. Pick up 2A, 3B, 4A, 2B, 1C, 1D, 1C, 2B, 4A, 3B, 1A, go with thread forward through the 1st and 2nd A beads just added in this step.

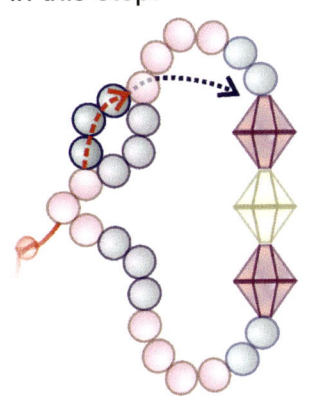

2. Pick up 3B, go with thread forward through the 1st A bead (of the 1st set of 4A) added in step #1.

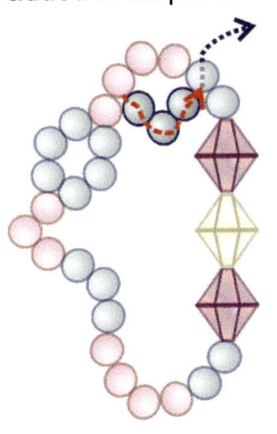

3. Pick up 3B, go with thread up through the 1st B bead (of the 1st set of 2B) added in step #1.

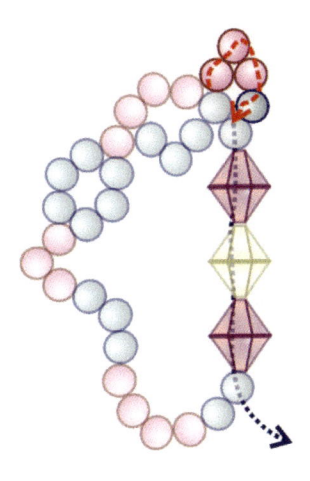

4. Pick up 3A, 1B, go with thread down through the 2nd B bead (of the 1st set of 2B), 1 C, 1 D, 1 C and the 1st B bead (of the 2nd set of 2B) added in step #1.

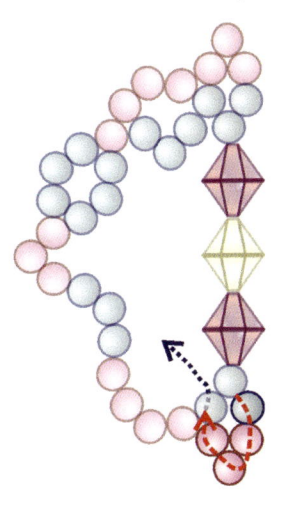

5. Pick up 1B, 3A, go with thread up through the 2nd B bead (of the 2nd set of 2B) added in step #1.

6. Pick up 3B, go with thread forward (up) through the 4th A bead (of the 2nd set of 4A) added in step #1.

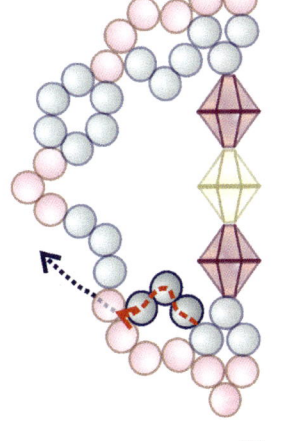

gold wine bracelet pattern 61

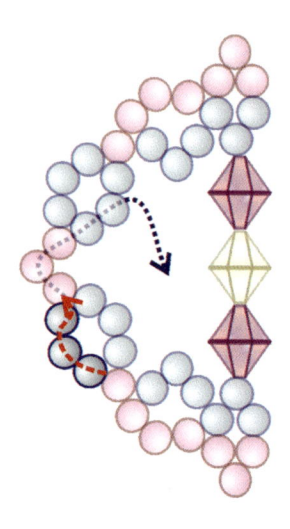

7. Pick up 3B, go with thread up through the last A bead, the 1st and 2nd A beads, added in step #1 and the 1st and 2nd B bead (of the 1st set of 3B) added in step #1.

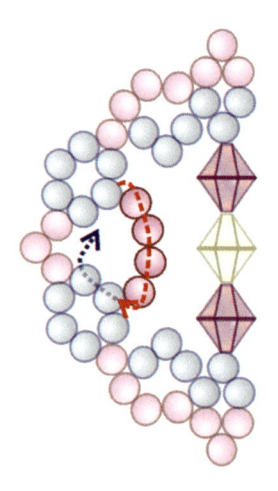

8. Pick up 4A, go with thread up through the 2nd and 3rd B bead (of the 2nd set of 3B) added in step #1.

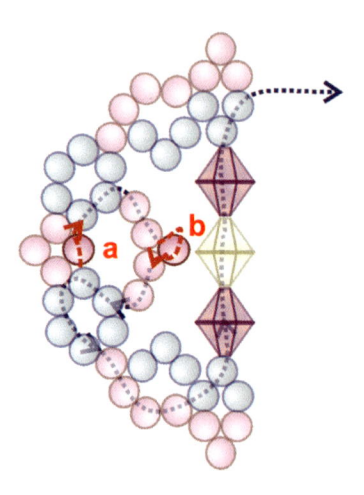

9. a) Pick up 1A, go with thread up through the 1st and 2nd B beads, (of the first set of 3B), step #1, and down through the 1st and 2nd A beads, step #8.
b) Pick up 1A, go with thread down through the 3rd and 4th A beads, step #8. Continue with working thread down then up through the beads as shown, coming out up through the B bead added in step #4.

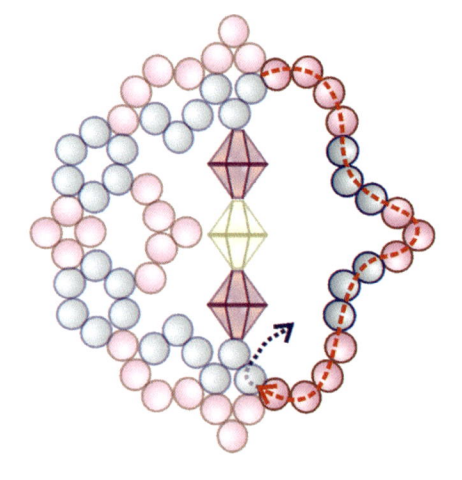

10. Pick up 4A, 3B, 3A, 3B, 4A, go with thread up through the B bead added in step #5 (FT), or step #16c (ETA).

62 beaded bracelets pattern collection

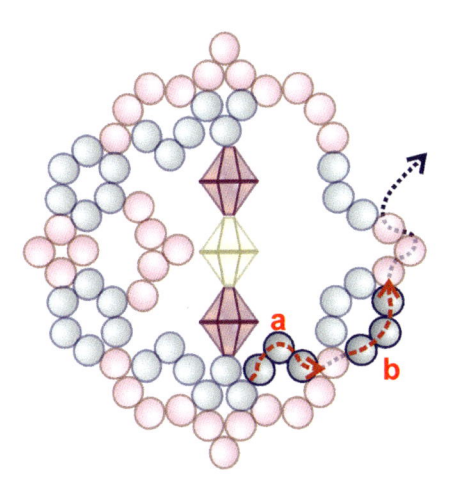

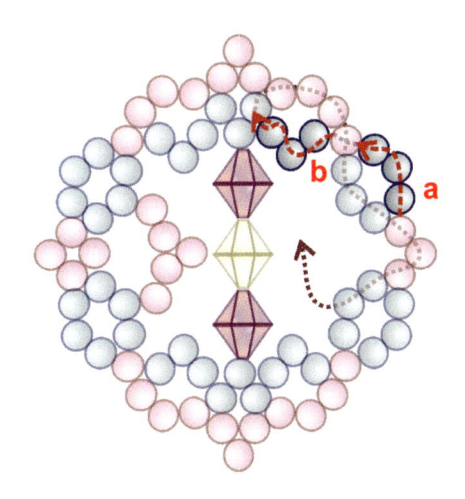

11. a) Pick up 3B, go with thread up through the 1st A bead (of the second set of 4A) added in step #10.
b) Pick up 3B, go with thread up through the 3 A beads (of the 3A) added in step #10.

12. a) Pick up 3B, go with thread up through the 4th A bead (of the 1st set of 4A) added in step #10.
b) Pick up 3B, go with thread up through the B bead added in step #4 (FT), or the step #16d (ETA), down through the 4 A, 3 B, 3 A, the 1st and 2nd B beads (of the second set of 3B) added in step #10.

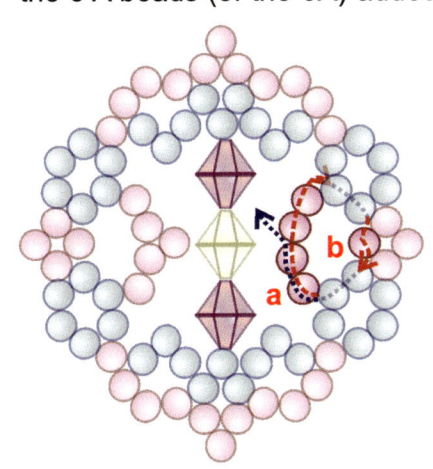

13. a) Pick up 4A, go with thread down through the 2nd and 3rd B beads (of the 1st set of 3B), step #10.
b) Pick up 1A, go with thread down through the 1st and 2nd B beads (of the 2nd set of 3B), step #10 and up through the 1st and 2nd A beads added in this step at (a).

14. Pick up 1A, go with thread up through the 3rd and 4th A beads, step #13a, down through the 2nd and 3rd B beads (of the 1st set of 3B) and the 1st and 2nd A beads (of the 3A) added in step #10.

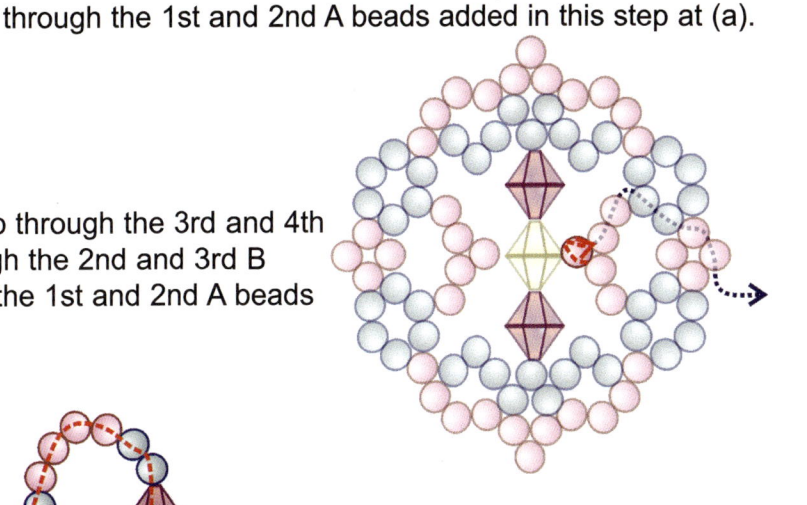

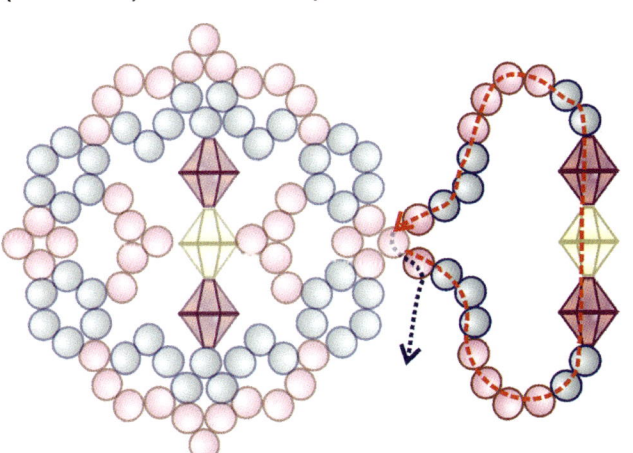

15. Pick up 1A, 3B, 4A, 2B, 1C, 1D, 1C, 2B, 4A, 3B, 1A, go with thread down through the 2nd A bead (of the 3A), step #10 and the 1st A bead just added in this step.

gold wine bracelet pattern 63

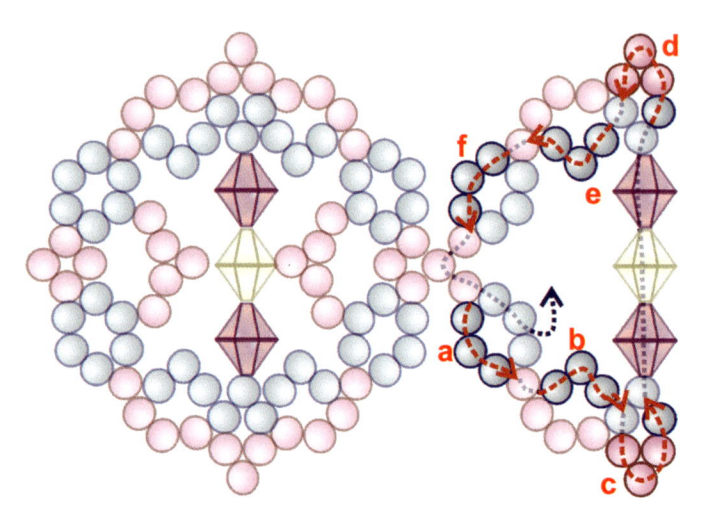

16. a) Pick up 3B, go with thread down through the 1st A bead (of the 1st set of 4A), step #15.
b) Pick up 3B, go with thread down through the 1st B bead (of the 1st set of 2B), step #15.
c) Pick up 3A, 1B, go with thread up through the 2nd B bead (of the 1st set of 2B), 1 C, 1 D, 1 C and the 1st B bead (of the 2nd set of 2B) added in step #15.
d) Pick up 1B, 3A, go with thread down though the 2nd B bead (of the 2nd set of 2B), step #15.
e) Pick up 3B, go with thread down through the 4th A bead (of the 2nd set of 4A), step #15.
f) Pick up 3B, go with thread down through the last A bead, step #15, the 2nd A bead, step #10, the 1st A bead, step #15 and the 1st and 2nd B beads (of the first set of 3B), step #15.

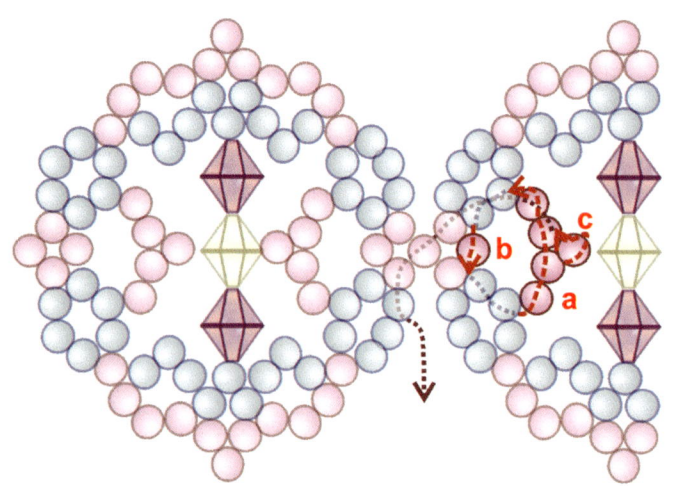

17. a) Pick up 4A, go with thread down through the 2nd and 3rd B beads (of the 2nd set of 3B), step #15.
b) Pick up 1A, go with thread down through the 1st and 2nd B beads (of the 1st set of 3B), step #15 and up through the 1st and 2nd A beads added in this step at (a).
c) Pick up 1A, go with thread up through the 3rd and 4th A beads, added in this step at (a), down through the 2nd and 3rd B beads (of the second set of 3B), step #15, the last A bead, step #15, the 2nd and 3rd A beads, step #10 and the 3rd B bead, step #11b.

18. Pick up 3B, go with thread up through the 1st B bead, step #16a, the 1st A bead, step #15, down through the 3rd A bead (of the 3A), step #10 and the 3 B beads, step #11b.

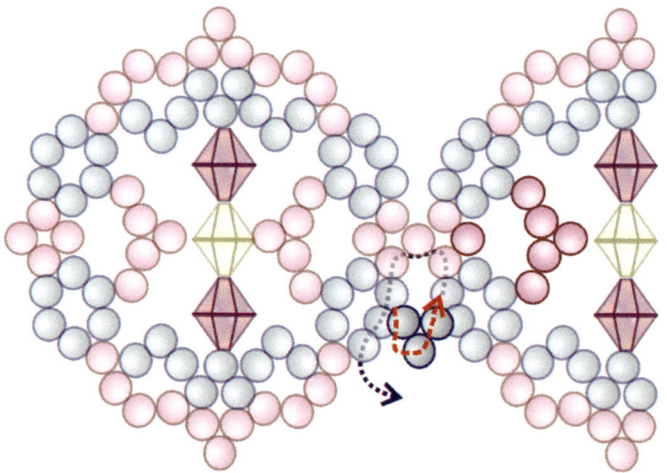

64 beaded bracelets pattern collection

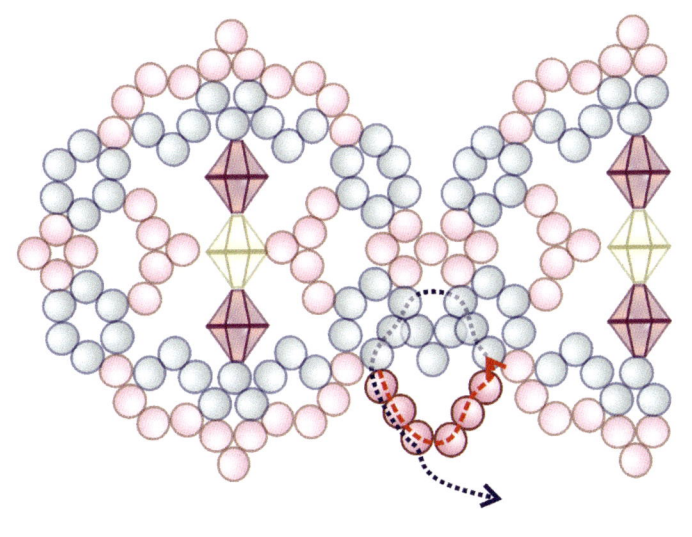

19. Pick up 6A, go with thread up through 3 B beads, step #16a, down through the 3 B bead, step #11b and the 1st, 2nd and 3rd A beads just added in this step.

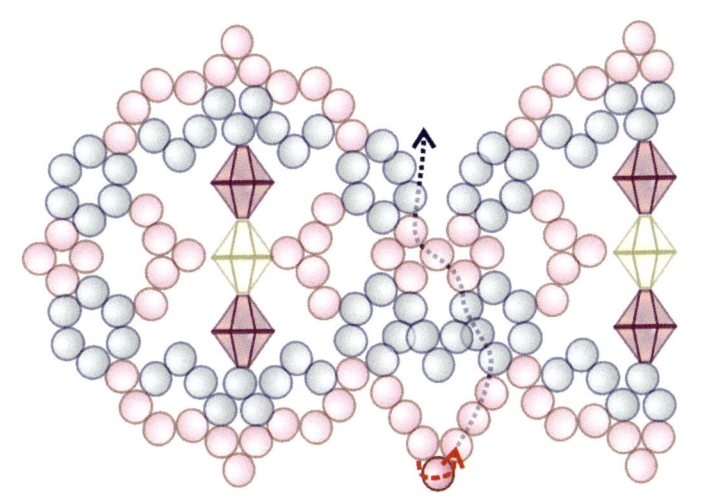

20. Pick up 1A, go with thread up through the bracelet as shown, coming out with working thread at the 1st B bead added in step #12a.

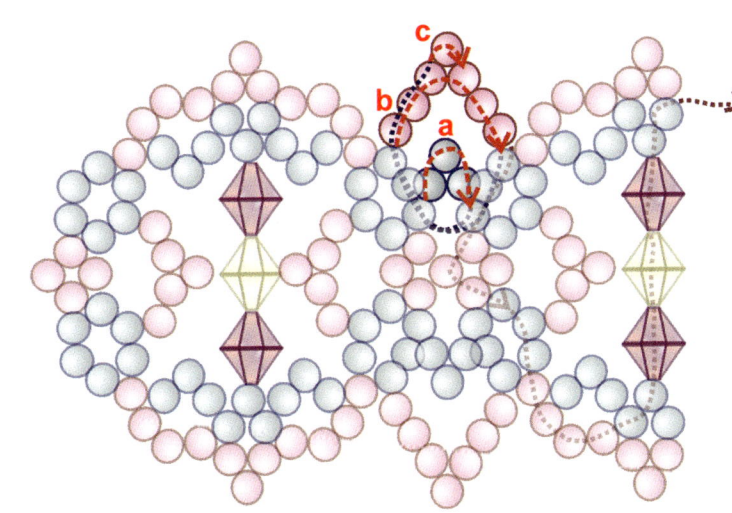

21. a) Pick up 3B, go with thread down through the 3rd B bead, step #16f and up through the 3 B beads, step #12a.
b) Pick up 6A, go with thread down through the 3 B beads, step #16f, up through the 3 B beads, #12a and the 1st, 2nd and 3rd A beads just added in this step.
c) Pick up 1A, go with thread down through the 4th, 5th and 6th A beads added in this step at (b). Continue with working thread down, then up, following the green thread path in illustration, coming out with working thread at the B bead added in step #16d.

gold wine bracelet pattern 65

22. Repeat steps #10 through #14.

23. Continue bracelet by repeating steps #15 through #22, until the bracelet fits.

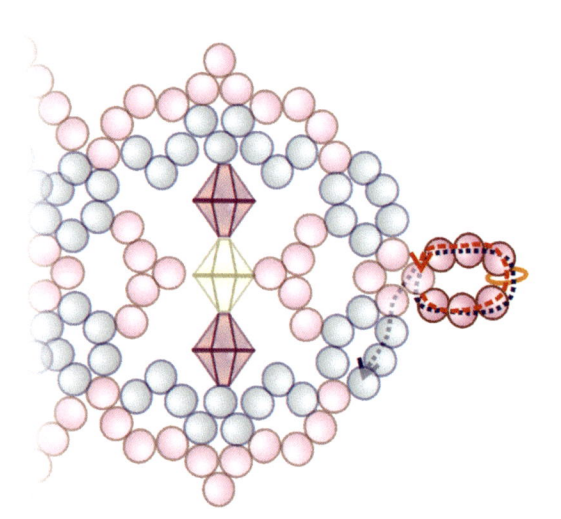

24. To add clasp, pick up 3A, clasp, 3A, go with thread down through 1 center bead in bracelet. Continue with working thread around through the clasp beads several times. Weave the working thread into the bracelet and end. Repeat the clasp directions in the same manner on the other end after removing the stopper bead.

66 beaded bracelets pattern collection

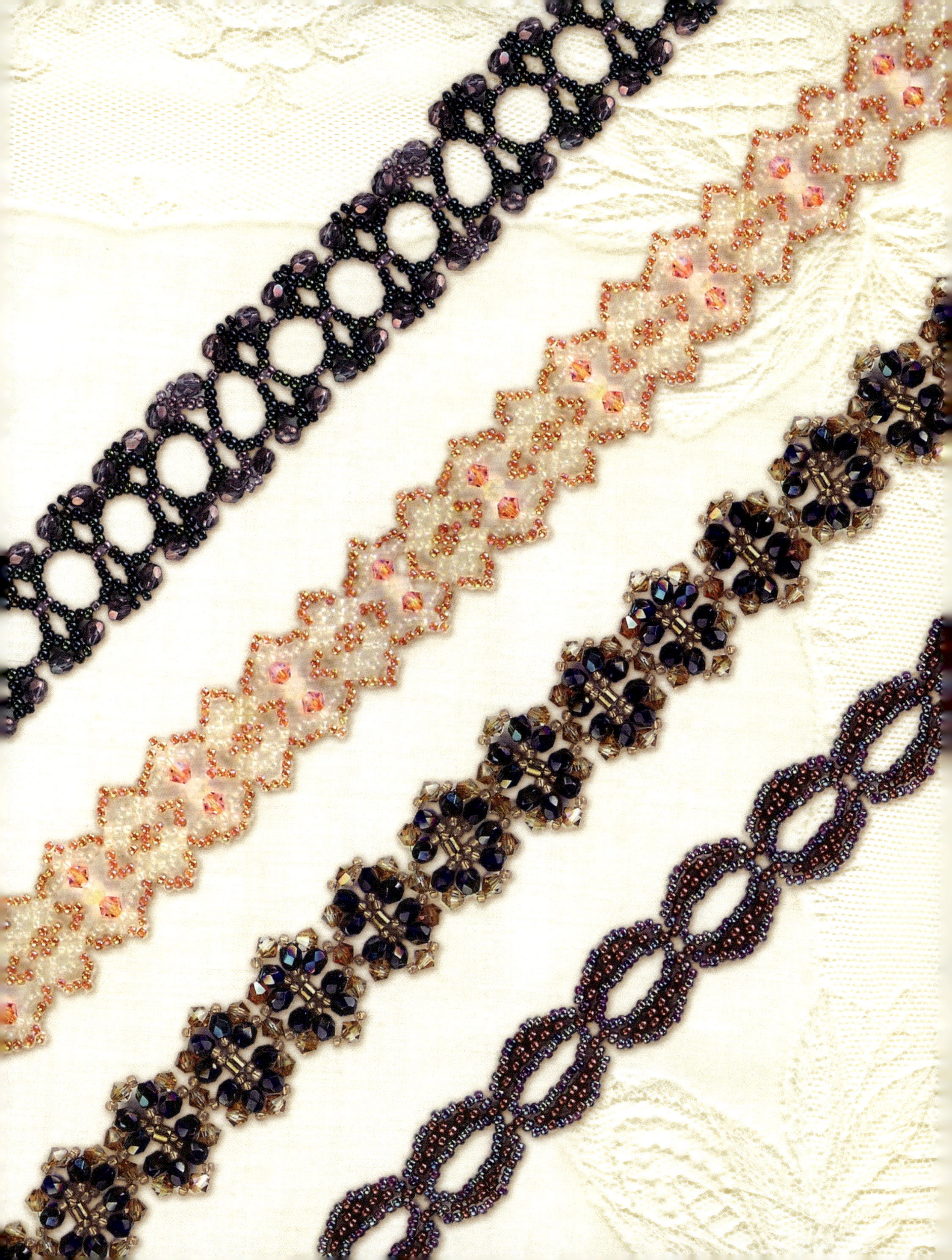

Crystal Explosion Bracelet

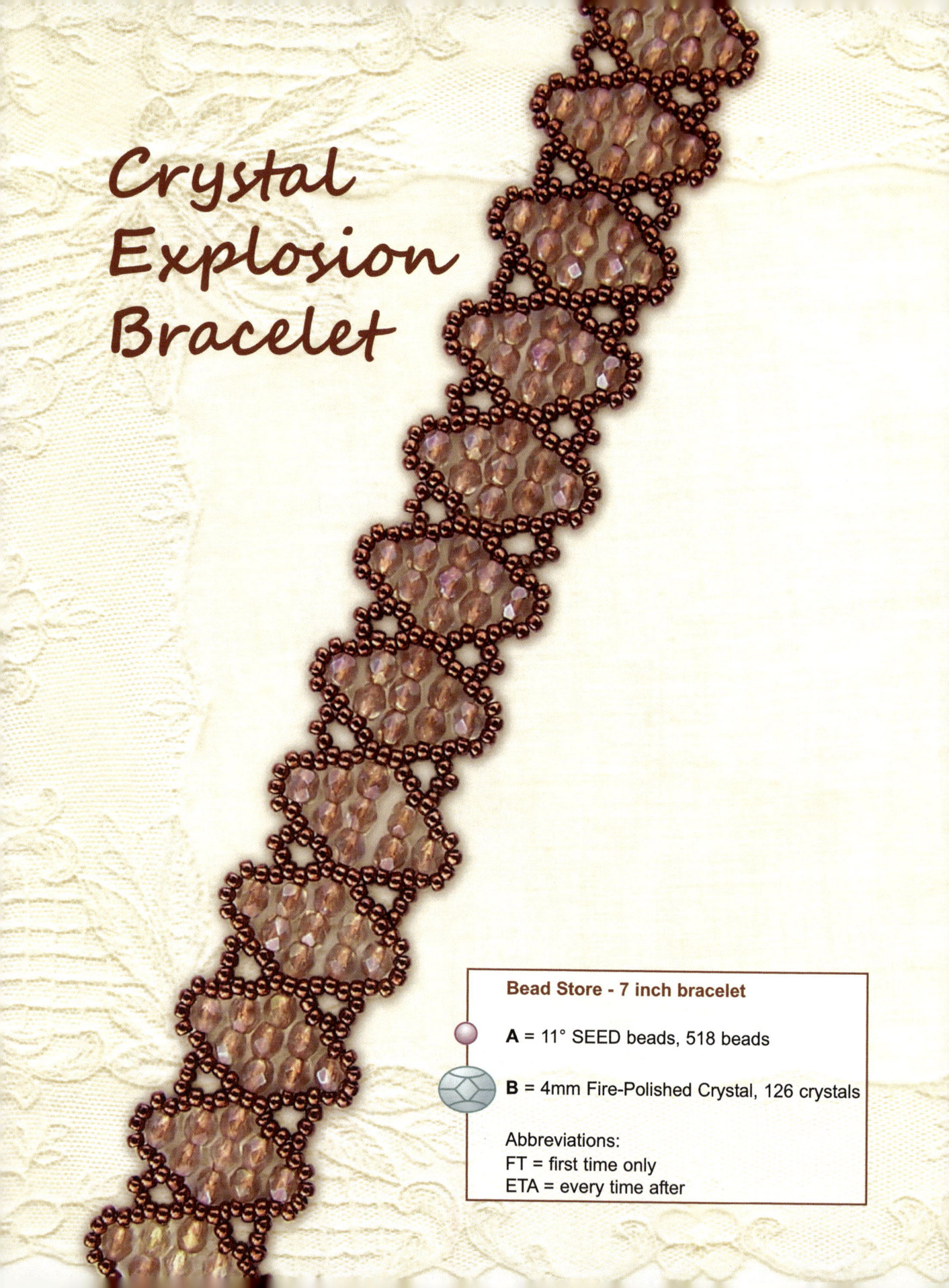

Bead Store - 7 inch bracelet

A = 11° SEED beads, 518 beads

B = 4mm Fire-Polished Crystal, 126 crystals

Abbreviations:
FT = first time only
ETA = every time after

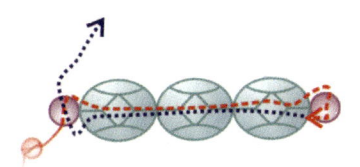

1. Pick up 1A, 3B, 1A, go with thread right to left through the 3 B beads just added and up (forward) through the 1st A bead just added in this step.

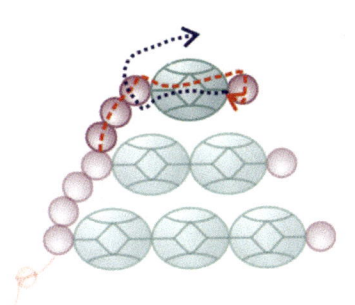

3. Pick up 3A, 1B, 1A, go with thread right to left through the 1 B bead just added and up (forward) through the 3rd A bead just added in this step.

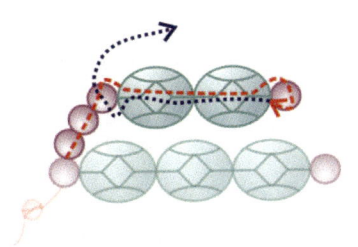

2. Pick up 3A, 2B, 1A, go with thread right to left through the 2 B beads just added and up (forward) through the 3rd A bead just added in this step.

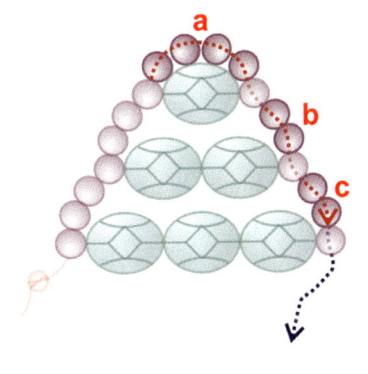

4. a) Pick up 4A, go with thread down through the last A bead, step #3.
b) Pick up 2A, go with thread down through the last A bead, step #2.
c) Pick up 2A, go with thread down through the last A bead, step #1.

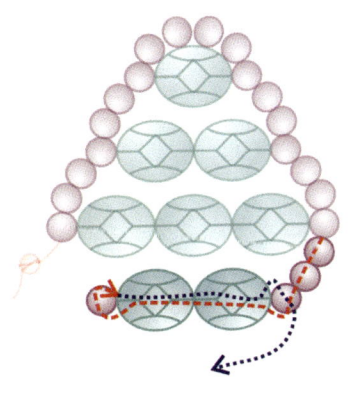

5. Pick up 3A, 2B, 1A, go with thread left to right through the 2 B beads just added and down (forward) through the 3rd A bead just added in this step.

crystal explosion bracelet pattern 69

6. Pick up 3A, 1B, 1A, go with thread left to right through the 1 B bead just added and down (forward) through the 3rd A bead just added in this step.

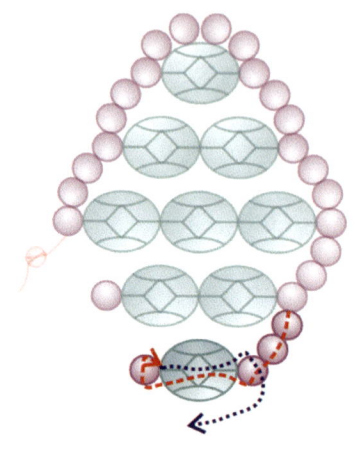

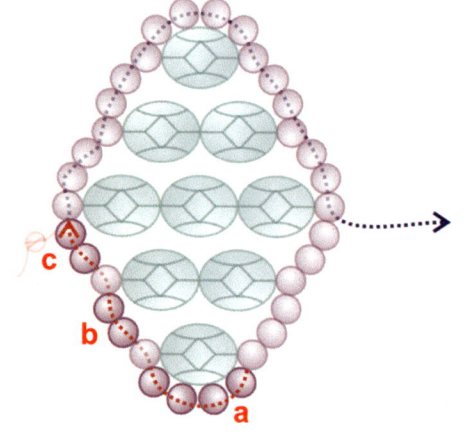

7. a) Pick up 4A, go with thread up through the last A bead, step #6.
b) Pick up 2A, go with thread up through the last A bead, step #5.
c) Pick up 2A, go with thread up through the 1st A bead, step #1. Continue with working thread by following the blue dotted line around through the outside A beads, coming out down through the last A bead, step #1.

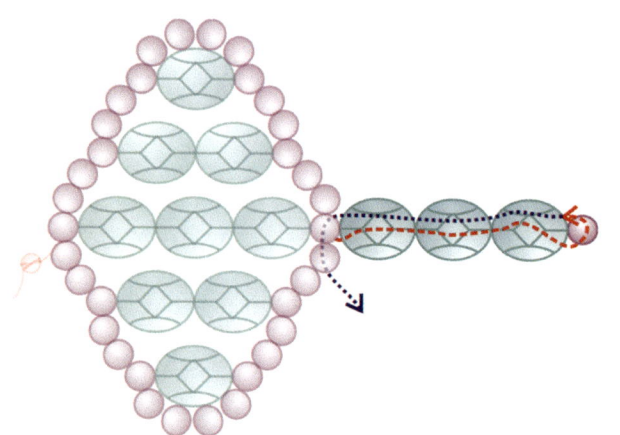

8. Pick up 3B, 1A, go with thread right to left through the 3 B beads just added in this step and down through the last A bead, step #1 (FT), or the 1 A bead, previous step #8 (ETA) and the 1st A bead, step #5 (FT), or the 2nd A bead, step #10c (ETA).

9. a) Pick up 2A, 2B, 1A, go with thread right to left through the 2 B beads just added and down (forward) through the 2nd A bead just added in this step.
b) Pick up 3A, 1B, 1A, go with thread right to left through the 1 B beads just added and down (forward) through the 3rd A bead just added in this step.

70 beaded bracelets pattern collection

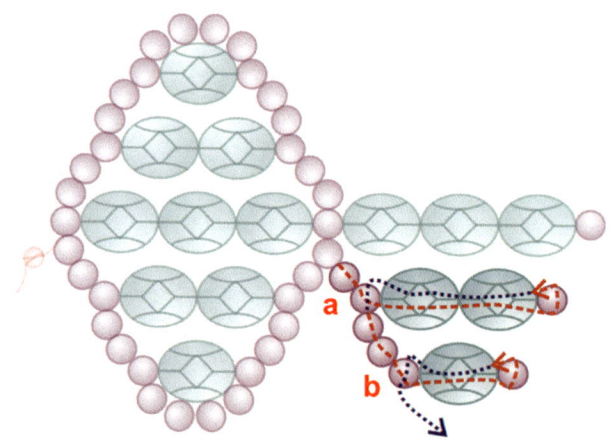

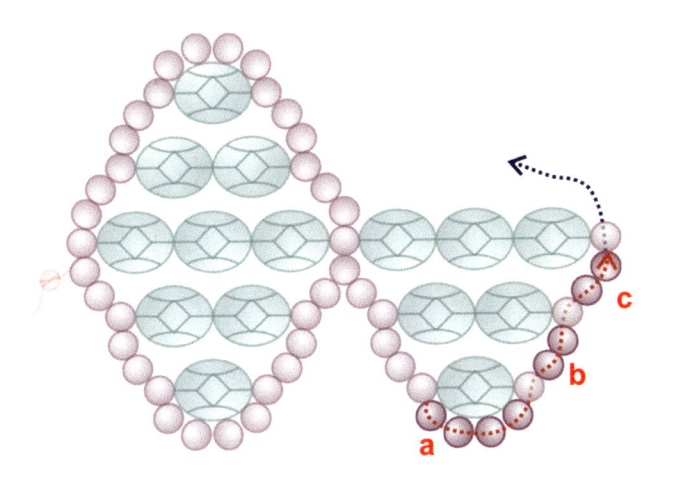

10. a) Pick up 4A, go with thread up through the last A bead, step #9b.
c) Pick up 2A, go with thread up through the last A bead, step #9a.
d) Pick up 2A, go with thread up through the 1st A bead, step #8.

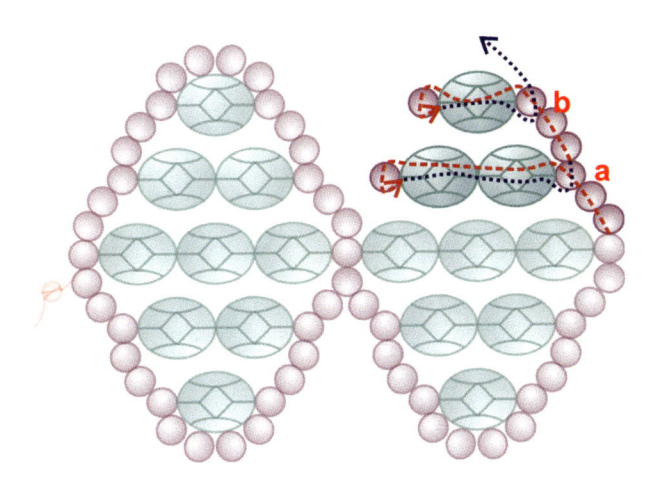

11. a) Pick up 3A, 2B, 1A, go with thread left to right through the 2 B beads just added and up (forward) through the 3rd A bead just added in this step.
b) Pick up 3A, 1B, 1A, go with thread left to right through the 1 B bead just added and up (forward) through the 3rd A bead just added in this step.

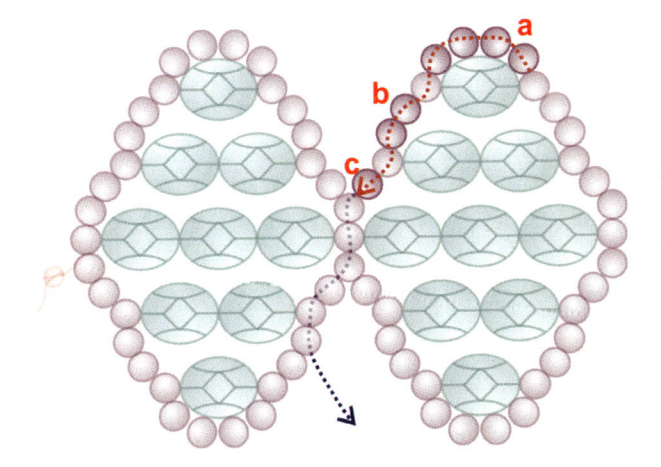

12. a) Pick up 4A, go with thread down through the last A bead, step #11b.
b) Pick up 2A, go with thread down through the last A bead, step #11a.
c) Pick up 1A, go with thread down through the 2nd A bead, step #4c and the 2nd A bead, step #1, 1st, 2nd and 3rd A beads, step #5, and the 1st A bead, step #6.

crystal explosion bracelet pattern

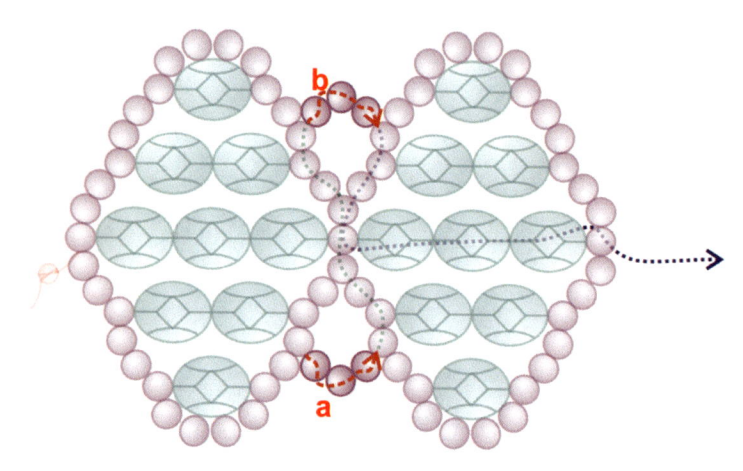

13. a) Pick up 3A, go with thread up through the 1st A bead, step #9b, the 2nd and 1st A beads, step #9a, the 1st A bead, step #5, the 2nd A bead, step #1, the 2 A beads, step #4c, the last A bead, step #2, and the 2nd A bead, step #4b.

b) Pick up 3A, go with thread down through the 2nd A bead, step #12b, the last A bead, step #11a, 1A bead, step #12c, the 2nd A bead, step #4c, the 2nd A bead, step #1, left to right through the 3 B beads and down through the 1 A bead, step #8.

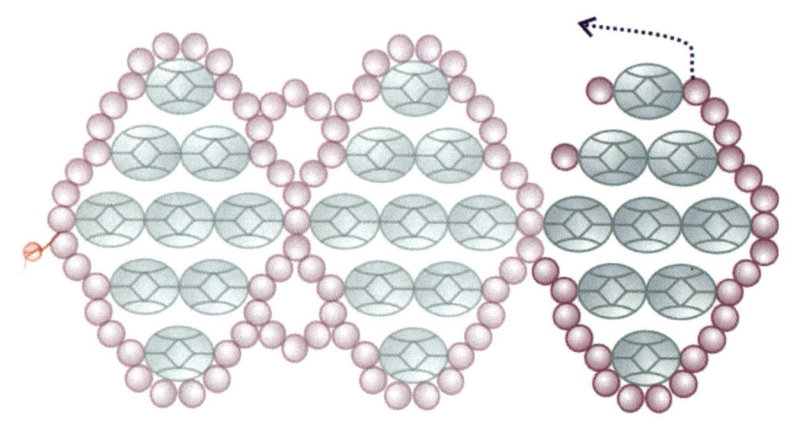

14. Repeat steps #8 through #11.

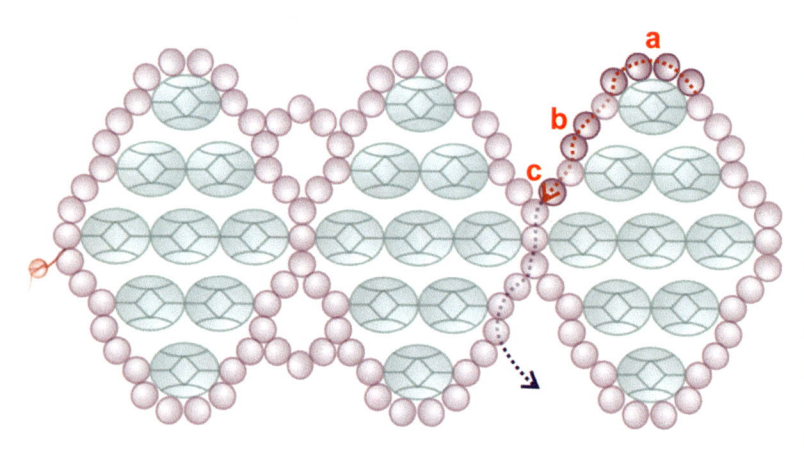

15. a) Pick up 4A, go with thread down through the last A bead, step #11b repeat.

b) Pick up 2A, go with thread down through the last A bead, step #11a repeat.

c) Pick up 1A, go with thread down through the 1st A bead, step #11a the 1 A bead, step #8, the 2 A beads, step #9a, the last A bead, step 39a and the 2nd A bead, step #10b.

72 beaded bracelets pattern collection

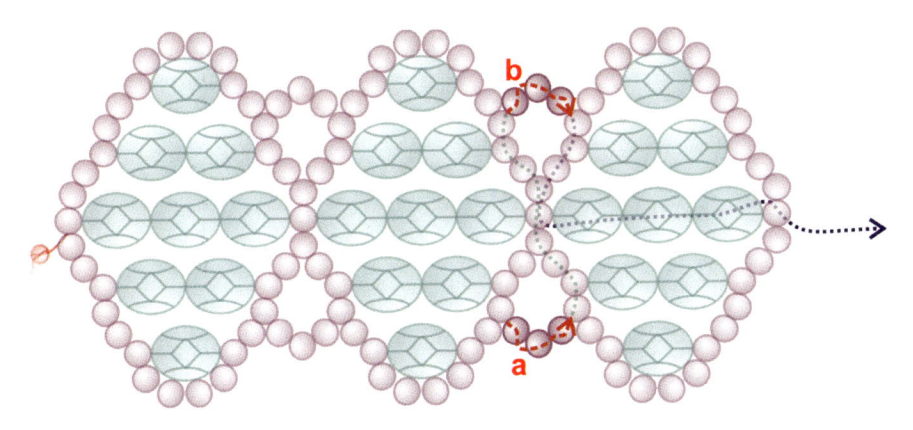

16. a) Pick up 3A, go with thread up through the 1st A bead, step #9b repeat, the 2nd and 1st A beads, step #9a repeat, the 2nd A bead, step #10c, the 1 A bead, step #8, the 1st, 2nd and 3rd A beads, step #11a, and the 1st A bead. step #11b.
b) Pick up 3A, go with thread down through the 2nd A bead, step #12b, the last A bead, step #11a, 1 A bead, step #12c, the 1st A bead, step #11a, the 1 A bead, step #8 previous repeat, left to right through the 3 B beads and down through the 1 A bead, step #8, working repeat.

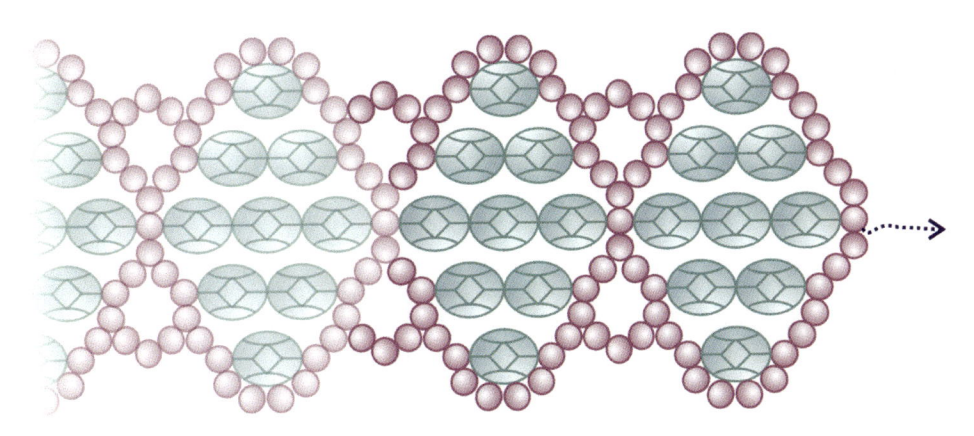

17. Continue bracelet by repeating steps #14 through #16, until the bracelet fits.

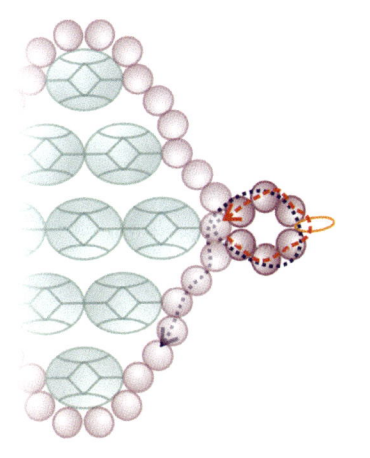

18. To add clasp, pick up 3A, clasp, 3A, go with thread down through 1 center bead in bracelet. Continue with working thread around through the clasp beads several times. Weave the working thread into the bracelet and end. Repeat the clasp directions in the same manner on the other end after removing the stopper bead.

crystal explosion bracelet pattern

Olive Lace Bracelet

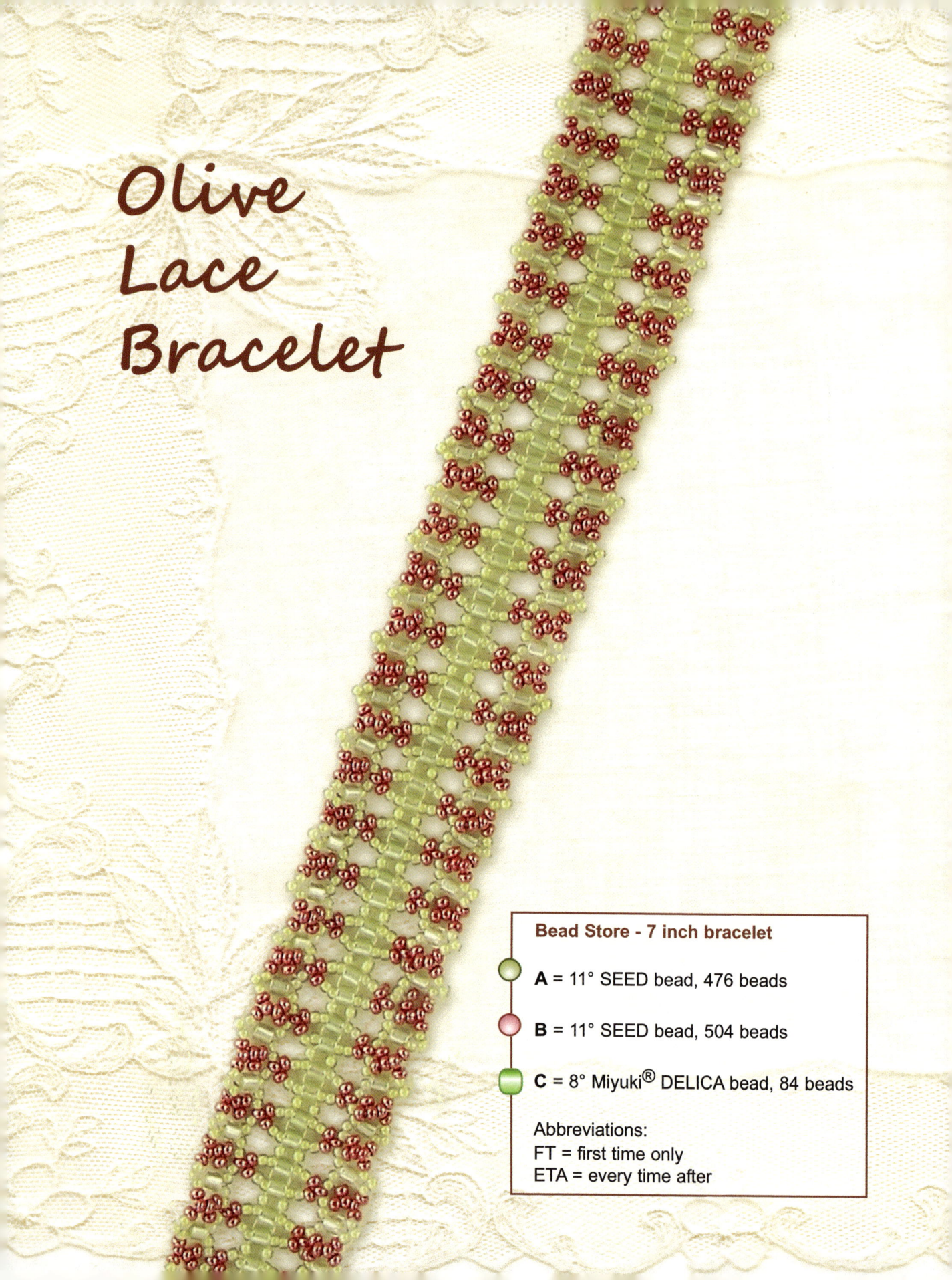

Bead Store - 7 inch bracelet

- **A** = 11° SEED bead, 476 beads
- **B** = 11° SEED bead, 504 beads
- **C** = 8° Miyuki® DELICA bead, 84 beads

Abbreviations:
FT = first time only
ETA = every time after

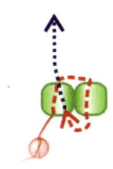

1. Pick up 2C, go with thread up through the 1st C bead just added.

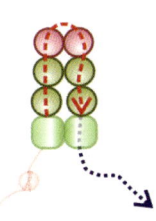

2. Pick up 2A, 2B, 2A, go with thread down through the 2nd C bead, step #1.

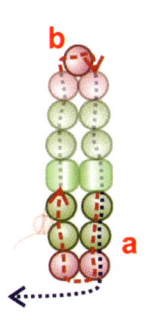

3. a) Pick up 2A, 2B, 2A, go with thread up through the 1st C bead, step #1, the first 2 A beads and the 1st B bead, step #2.
b) Pick up 1B, go with thread down through the 2nd B and the last 2 A beads, step #2, the 2nd C bead, step #1, the first 2 A and 1st B beads added in this step at (a).

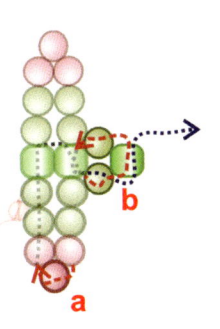

4. a) Pick up 1B, go with thread up through the 2nd B bead and the second set of 2 A beads, step #3a, the 1st C bead and down through the 2nd C bead, step #1.
b) Pick up 1A, 1C, 1A, go with thread down through the 2nd C bead, step #1 (FT) or the 1 C bead, step #5 (ETA), forward through the 1st A bead and up through the 1 C bead just added in this step.

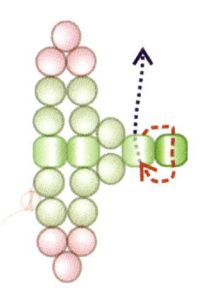

5. Pick up 1C, go with thread up through the C bead, step #4b.

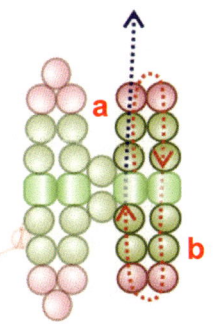

6. a) Pick up 2A, 2B, 2A, go with thread down through the C bead, step #5.
b) Pick up 2A, 2B, 2A, go with thread up through the C bead, step #4b, the first 2 A beads and the 1st B bead added in this step at (a).

olive lace bracelet pattern 75

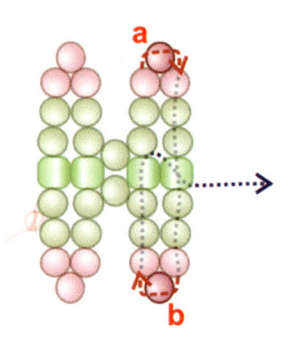

7. a) Pick up 1B, go with thread down through the 2nd B and the last 2 A beads, step #6a, the C bead, step #5, the first 2 A and 1st B beads, step #6b.
b) Pick up 1B, go with thread up through the 2nd B bead and the second set of 2 A beads, step #6B, the C bead, step #4b and down through the C bead, step #5.

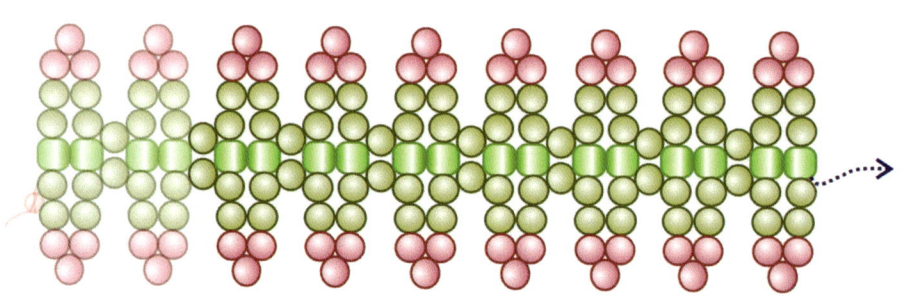

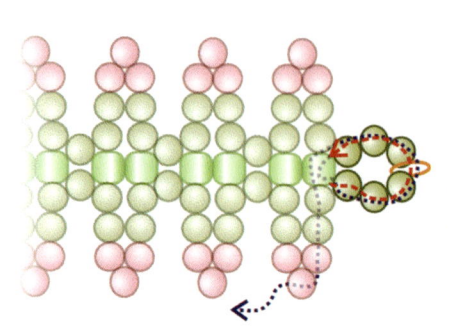

8. Repeat steps #4b through #7 until you reach the length that you would like your bracelet to be.

9. To add clasp, pick up 3A, clasp, 3A, go with thread down through 1 center C bead in bracelet. Continue with working thread around through the clasp beads several times. Weave the working thread down through 2 A and 1 B beads as shown, and right to left through the 1 B bead added in the repeat of step #7b.

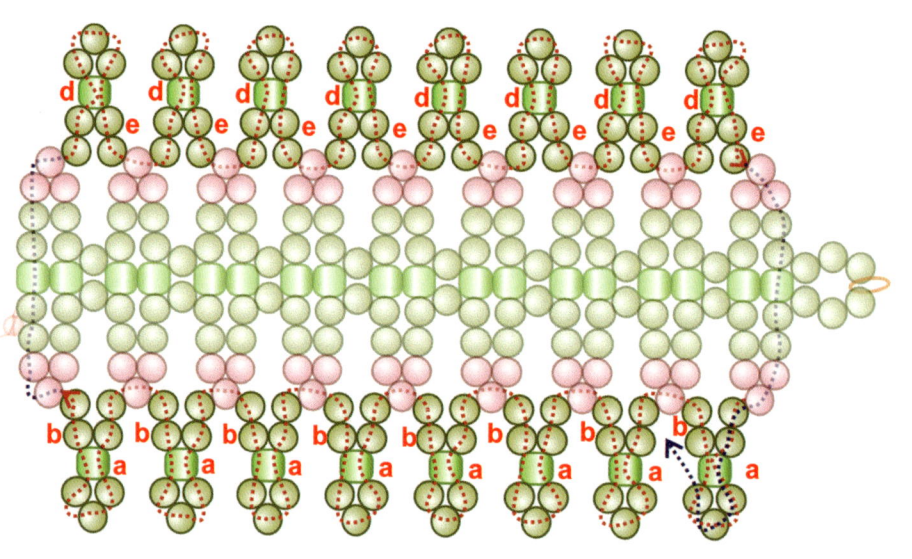

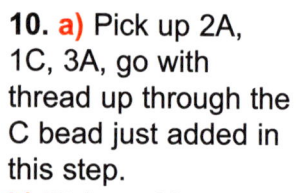

10. a) Pick up 2A, 1C, 3A, go with thread up through the C bead just added in this step.
b) Pick up 2A, go with thread right to left through the 1 B bead, step #7b repeat to the left.
c) Repeat (a and b) right to left along the bottom of the bracelet as shown. Continue with working thread up through the beads on the side of the bracelet, coming out with thread left to right through the 1 B bead added in step #3b.
d) Pick up 2A, 1C, 3A, go with thread down through the C bead just added in this step.
e) Pick up 2A, go with thread left to right through the 1 B bead, step #7a repeat to the right.
f) Repeat (d and e) left to right along the top of the bracelet as shown. Continue with working thread down through the beads on the right side of the bracelet, coming out with thread around and forward through the 3 A beads added in this step at (a).

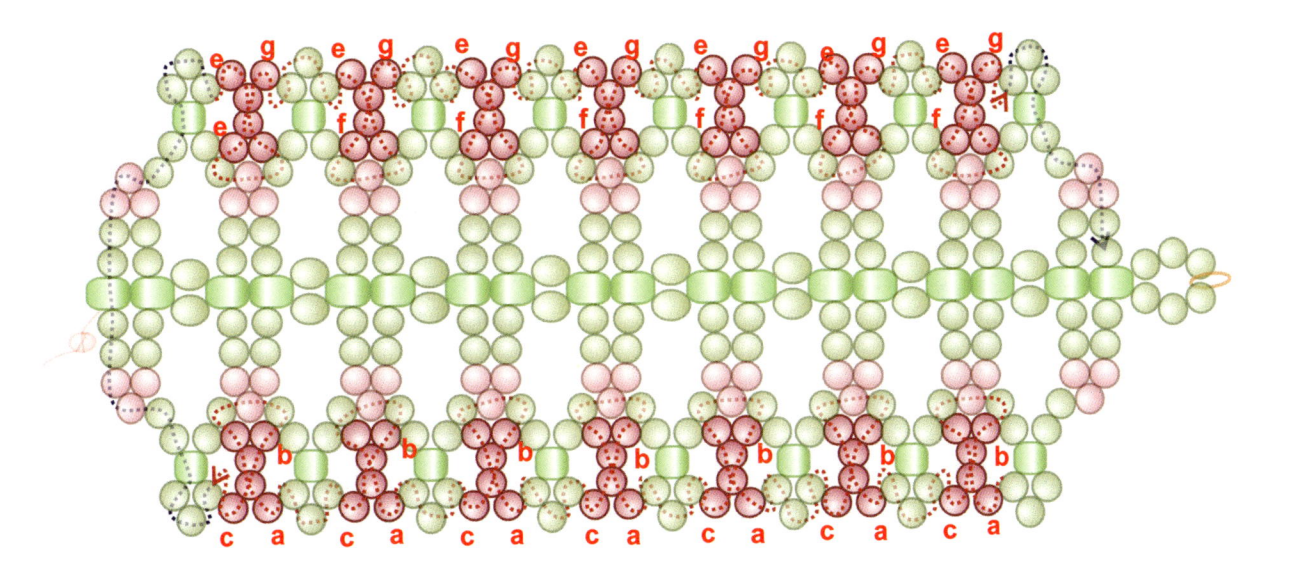

11. a) Pick up 4B, go with thread left to right through the 1st A bead, step #10a, repeat on left, the 1 B bead, step #7b, and the 2nd A bead, step #10b, repeat on the right.
b) Pick up 1B, go with thread down through the 3rd and 2nd B beads added in this step at (a).
c) Pick up 1B, go with thread right to left through the set of 3B beads, Step #10a, repeat right.
d) Repeat (a, b, c) right to left along the bottom of the bracelet as shown. Continue with working thread up through the beads on the left side of the bracelet, coming out with thread left to right through the set of 3A beads added in step #10d.
e) Pick up 4B, go with thread right to left through the 1st A bead, step #10d, repeat on right, the 1 B bead, step #7a, and the 2nd A bead, step #10e, repeat on the left.
f) Pick up 1B, go with thread up through the 3rd and 2nd B beads added in this step at (e).
g) Pick up 1B, go with thread left to right through the set of 3B beads, Step #10d, repeat right.
h) Repeat (e, f, g) left to right along the top of the bracelet as shown. Weave the working thread into the bracelet and end.

12. Remove the stopper bead. Put the end thread onto a needle and pick up 3A, clasp, 3A, go with thread down through 1 center C bead in bracelet. Continue with working thread around through the clasp beads several times. Weave the working thread into the bracelet and end.

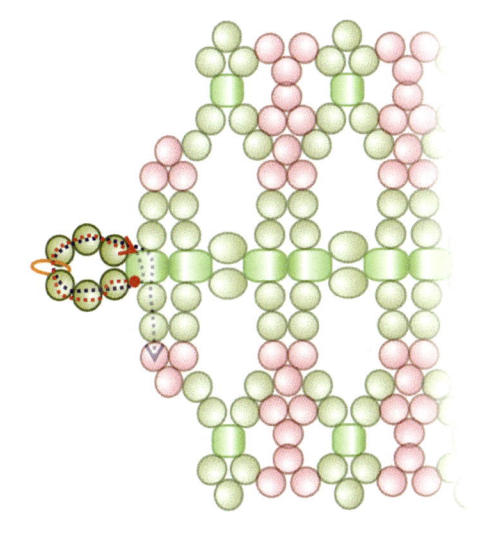

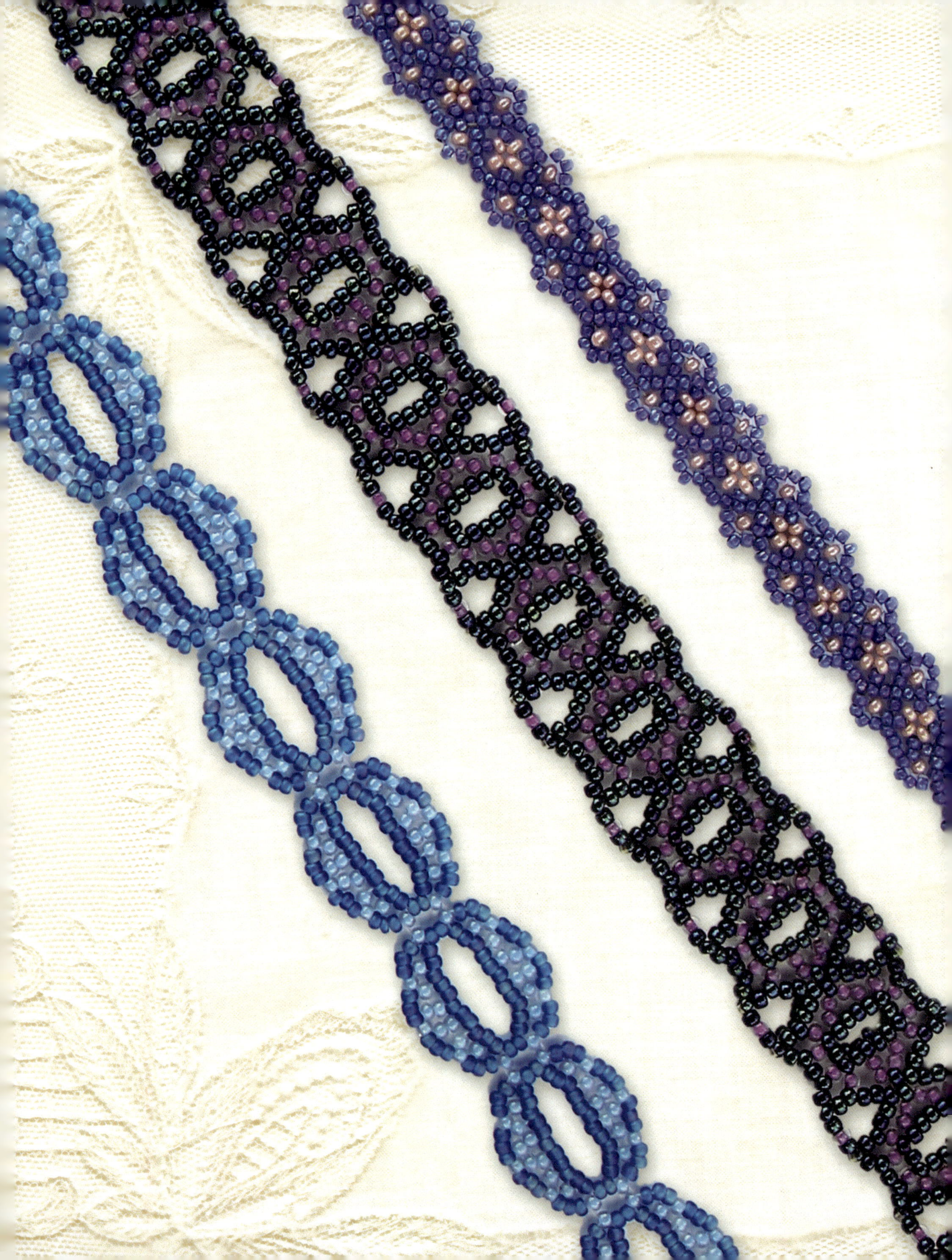

Made in the USA
Lexington, KY
20 May 2013